Sharing F... W9-CEV-677

"A GREAT RESOURCE for individuals and church groups."
—PUBLISHERS WEEKLY

"FACED WITH A WORLD where 1.1 billion people lack enough calories to ward off hunger, and 1.1 billion persons struggle with obesity, L. Shannon Jung demonstrates the noble art of both eating and sharing. Practical Christian theology at its best, this book affirms life, avoids the shaming game, and awards readers with new pathways to discover the spiritual joy of food."

—DONALD E. MESSER
President, Center for the Church and Global AIDS,
co-author of *Ending Hunger Now*

"IN THE DIN of contemporary market voices for a sea of products we consume without any real or lasting joy, here comes a little volume that calls us back to simple, joyful practices over what really sustains our lives—our food. In an era that's long discounted religious ritual to the point of forgetting the most basic of moral and ethical acts, here is a vital voice for meaningful, practiced sharing, grace, hospitality, feasting, cooking, fasting. Our hearts yearn for answers, hope, and direction in a dark and hungry world. L. Shannon Jung's *Sharing Food* warmly responds, lighting our path home."

—TONY ENDS
Director, Churches' Center for Land and People,
and family farmer

Sharing Food

CHRISTIAN PRACTICES FOR ENJOYMENT

L. SHANNON JUNG

FORTRESS PRESS
MINNEAPOLIS

For all those, like me,

who fight being overweight because

they love sharing food

SHARING FOOD
Christian Practices for Enjoyment

Cover image: El Pan Nuestro 1923–28 Diego Rivera (1886–1957). Painting © The Banco de Mexico Diego Rivera and Frida Kahlo Museums Trust. Photo © ET Archive London / SuperStock. Used by permission.
Cover design: Laurie Ingram
Book design: Ann Delgehausen / Trio Bookworks

Library of Congress Cataloging-in-Publication Data
Jung, L. Shannon (Loyle Shannon), 1943-
    Sharing food : Christian practices for enjoyment / by L. Shannon Jung.
        p. cm.
    ISBN-13: 978-0-8006-3792-7 (alk. paper)
    ISBN-10: 0-8006-3792-5 (alk. paper)
    1. Food—Religious aspects—Christianity. I. Title.
    BR115.N87J87 2006
    248.4'6—dc22

                                    2006012788

The paper used in this publication meets the minimum requirements of American National Standard for Information Sciences—Permanence of Paper for Printed Library Materials, ANSI Z329.48-1984.

Manufactured in the U.S.A.

Contents

Preface

THIS IS A BOOK ABOUT LEARNING to eat well.

Does that mean it is a diet book? Well, yes and no. If by "diet book" we mean a heavily regimented series of dos and don'ts about how to lose weight, this is not a diet book. But if we mean a book about diet, or how to eat healthily and happily, this is definitely a diet book. It is tailored to fit the way God designed us to be. So it is a super diet book. As a matter of fact, following the seven Christian practices described in this book will probably mean that we will lose weight. More important, we will learn to enjoy eating by practicing these activities. We will come to enjoy our lives by sharing ourselves as well as food with others. So this is a book about eating with *jouissance*, with overflowing joy.

My earlier book *Food for Life: The Spirituality and Ethics of Eating* (Fortress Press, 2004) serves as a biblical and theological foundation for this one. Having written about personal and global eating disorders there, I felt pressure to explore *how* everyday eating practices could contribute to delight and sharing, the twin purposes for which God designed eating. I found those practices in the spiritual vault of the tradition and have updated them for us in the twenty-first century.

This book could help us discover the path toward eating enjoyably. That, in turn, will lead us to thank God for our daily bread and to see even the preparing of meals as a spiritual practice. The practices described below will help us get in touch with God—or allow us to be open to God's getting in touch with us. The following chapters offer activities that take us out of our chairs and into the world. In that way the book is quite practical.

Groups could profitably study the book—either in an academic classroom or an adult education class. I intend to put faith into action and uncover the links between belief and practice. Because I have tried to balance theology and praxis, this book would fit into a course on moral issues or Christian ethics, or theology, or even into a biblical studies course. Students and other adult learners will appreciate its concreteness and practicability.

It is my great pleasure to acknowledge the contributions made to this book by a large number of audiences, in classrooms, church meetings, and private conversations. The Lutheran Academy of the Rockies was an exceptional venue that gave me a chance to hear responses to five lectures in ten days. I have tested this manuscript in presbytery meetings, gatherings of scholars, and academic classrooms as well.

Students have given me a wonderful range of responses. I thank those in my Theology of Eating class at the University of Dubuque Seminary and Wartburg Seminary, and in the Spirituality and the Renewal of Rural Congregations class at Saint Paul School of Theology, Kansas City. Pat Sileo, Rob Brink, and Arleen Cairo scrutinized the manuscript and gave sage, blunt, and incisive opinions. Thomas Schattauer and Gordon Lathrop guided me through the discussion of the Eucharist (chapter 8). Jeanne Hoeft at Saint Paul School of Theology saved me from a number of psychological gaffes.

I asked two educational curriculum specialists to work with me on the "practical" sections at the conclusion of chapters 2–8: Ann Boltinghouse and Kathy Bonn were able to shape those in ways that make the practices live. Nancy Barry, a writing specialist and English professor at Luther College, made great suggestions to improve the flow of the book. Julie Phillips at the Center for Theology and Land was a whiz on the computer and made numerous helpful comments along the way.

It is a lot to ask colleagues to read one's manuscript critically, especially if they are conscientious people. My friends and colleagues Pamela Couture, Dean at Saint Paul; Patricia Beattie Jung, Loyola University in Chicago; and Craig Nessan, Dean at Wartburg Seminary, were simply unbelievable. Bless you, bless you, bless you.

I have really enjoyed working with Michael West, Bob Todd, Laurie Ingram, and Abby Hartman at Fortress Press; they are a quality outfit.

God has richly blessed me with a zesty, even piquant family, great colleagues and friends, good restaurants, and a superb life partner. Thank you all.

Introduction:
How Can We Eat Well?

WE FACE AN UNPRECEDENTED PROBLEM with food in the United States. There is too much of it. What should we do with it? How do we dispose of all those calories?

One way we do that is pretty obvious to any observer. We carry them around our waists, our hips, our bellies, and our bottoms. That, of course, produces other problems: respiratory disease, heart attacks, and diabetes, as well as their more common precursors: shortness of breath, inability to move freely, and general fatigue. Let me tell you, these are real issues for many of us.

Some of those excess calories are infused into almost every meal. Michael Pollan claims that there are five hundred extra calories produced every day for every man, woman, and child in this country. We manage to use two hundred of those calories by processing them into soft drinks, alcohol, prepared foods (ready to heat and eat), and snacks.[1] But that produces other problems.

Even poor people, especially poor people in this country, do their share—indeed, more than their share—to dispose of those calories. Part of that has to do with the cheapness of food that is unhealthy, although it tastes great. It is hard for me to resist potato chips, for example, or Twinkies.

This adds yet another layer to the conundrum. Seldom, if ever, has any civilization had such a wealth of great food. Indeed, the availability of wonderful foods feeds into our propensity to eat away our fears or restlessness or vulnerability. Eating is for many of us our default position, the way we ease our anxiousness or frame our difficulties.

All of this produces an approach-avoidance situation. We regard eating both as a problem and a great joy. What feeds us also makes us sick. What gladdens our souls can bring disorder and excess as well. So we often spend a lot of money to lessen the excess. The more money we throw at the problems produced by too much—diet books, slimming products, medicines, and TV shows—the worse they seem to become. There are multimillion dollar businesses tied into our tendency to consume too much. This is puzzling. Our solutions, rather than curing our illnesses, seem to inflame them. The more we know about the dangers of overeating and eating unwisely, the more we eat. And yet eating is still a great joy.

There is another unprecedented problem with food as well, the problem of distribution. We know the consequences of having too much, too many calories. We used to assume that those who had money were well nourished, but that may no longer be true. Many of us are poorly nourished as well as overnourished. Yet there continue to be those who don't have enough money or food. In fact, their numbers may be growing. Even in a country awash in food, there are 35 million who are "food insecure." Hurricane Katrina vividly revealed the lengths to which people will go when they don't have enough food or water. The fact of hunger both worldwide and here at home is another burden for those who think it offensive that in a world with enough food, some starve.

How can we sort out how to eat in a way that is healthy and cuts through these problems? How can we really enjoy our food rather than seeing it as a problem? In short, how can we eat well? This book offers an answer to that question, one that has to do with learning Christian eating practices.

Rather than worrying about what we eat or working obsessively at controlling our eating, these practices offer us a way of appreciating food. This book aims to help us eat more mindfully and to celebrate the simple joy of daily eating. Not only that, it shows how eating can help us get in touch with God. God offers us a daily abundance of good things, including food and each other. Participating in activities that transcend unconscious routines can help us realize the goodness of life. It may be that this is one way we put ourselves in a place to sense God's getting in touch with us.

The Christian message witnesses to the delight found in sharing with others. One might even say that it is difficult to really delight when one cannot share. Learning to share deeply with others is a practice that takes real mindfulness today, some of that counter-cultural. The good news is that we can learn to love and delight in hospitality. This book will describe and update some time-honored eating practices that make for joy in eating and in Christian community. I suggest ways we can learn how to eat well.

The Significance of Spiritual Practices

The spiritual practices I have been referring to might seem somewhat elevated or reserved only for the superpious. That is not my intention. Rather, these are time-proven behaviors that can save ordinary Christians from either overdecision (having to think through every decision) or moral relativism. They are objective ways of acting, which the Christian movement has found can lead us into satisfying relationships with other people, ourselves, God, and nature. They deal with perennial questions of life. As such, they have the power to transform us and even to offer us a haven in an anxious world. This means that most spiritual practices also have moral dimensions.

Furthermore, these spiritual and moral practices are important because people who participate in them express a common loyalty. The practices are "acted meanings." They embody certain beliefs about the world, and we find that our conscious beliefs are changed by these practices just as our practices are adopted because of our beliefs. These beliefs and practices are shared by many. As a result, they form and inform community. While it is possible in an individualistic culture such as ours to live to ourselves or in small groups, the practices discussed here are inherently corporate. They have the power to form community, a much-needed antidote to the fragmentation we feel and the overwhelming powerlessness that massive societal issues engender, for example, world hunger or global economics.

Practices are fluid carriers of meaning that can be shaped to accommodate new features of context within their traditional forms. As they beckon individual men and women to associations that carry shared meanings, they are capable of being appropriated for particular communities.

Larry Rasmussen talks both about master practices (like baptism) and ancillary practices (like producing water bottles inscribed with the mission or logo of a particular group such as Holden Village, Montreat, IBM, or Youth Leadership School).[2] Pastor Rachel Hanson tells the story of a giant pumpkin grown by a little girl named Anna. The pumpkin was so big that it remained unbought at a church auction held to raise funds. The next week people in the church decided to cut up the pumpkin and make bars, cakes, and pies out of it. They sold the produce and gave the money to Lutheran World Relief to relieve world hunger! When they do the same thing next year, it will become the ancillary practice of Anna's pumpkin. Most congregations are capable of inventing analogous practices that are both fun and community building.

There is another reason why spiritual practices are important today. They empower the individual, the small group, and voluntary associations such as the church to act in the face of injustice and suffering. To be sure, we hope to have a societal impact through spiritual practices such as buying foods locally or honoring bodily fitness, but perhaps it is just as important to foster morally commendable actions and to build communities of solidarity and resistance. For example, the simple practice of saying grace can promote humility and also remind us of the injustices that result in others' hunger. It is refreshing to the human spirit to live in shared, deliberate ways that may run counter to the majority culture. Indeed, sharing may be one way of witnessing to the joy of eating.

Sharing Food

It could be argued that sharing food is the central Christian spiritual practice when it comes to eating. Why sharing? Why not relishing, or relinquishing? The easiest way to illustrate why this might be so is to tell a story.

Winters are cold in Minnesota, and it is not a hospitable climate for the homeless. The Dorothy Day House in Moorhead, Minnesota, provided not only warmth and food but as close to a home for transients and the homeless as was possible.

On Saturdays I used to take our two boys—ages eight and ten or so—over there to fix lunch and talk to whoever was living there. We got over our initial hesitancy and usually had a pretty good time fixing and serving lunch, cleaning up, and then visiting. What I will always remember as the best part, however, was the feeling I got on the way home: "This thing we have just done was really worthwhile. This was worth doing, and doing together." That was the feeling. Our work met some deep need of ours and was something we did for ourselves more than for the folks at the House. We relished the opportunity to share. We celebrated having and sharing food. I cannot say we salivated over the opportunity, but you get the point. Sharing was enjoyable in a profound sense.

I am convinced that we have a deep need to share. We experience real joy in sharing. It may take a little practice, and we may need to get over our initial hesitancy to let go rather than to pursue and clutch. But the rewards are immense. Indeed, all the evidence suggests that God created us with certain purposes and drives that crave to be satisfied. God created us with the instincts to seek not only our own well-being but that of others as well. Each creature would pursue its own well-being within the well-being of the whole. Call it the Hebraic vision of *shalom*. The promise is that there is enough for all creatures. We have a capability for *jouissance*—for joy!

Is this not what we really want? We want to be deeply contented, to be connected with others, to be satisfied, to enjoy as fully as our human constitution will allow and to enjoy in a way that others can enjoy as well. Do you remember those times with friends when everything was clicking and everyone was relaxed and secure with everybody else enough to let down, when each of you was *ubuntu* (the Swahili word for having one's own well-being increased by the other's well-being)? Isn't that the gusto we want to grab? Sometimes it just feels *ṣaddîq* (the Hebrew word for "just" or "right"). The forces of the universe line up in us, and we know we are *ṣaddîq*.

But we seem to live in a culture of fear today. Our lives are increasingly governed by security-consciousness, as any airline traveler can attest. We tout our empirelike power, but it does little to secure our future or to render daily life more joy-filled. Indeed, in our hide-your-faults, deny-your-failures culture, we seem increasingly controlled by the fears we have trouble confessing. The cost of hiding fear is high. Furthermore, what Katrina blew away was our illusion that we could somehow protect ourselves from any eventuality.

What I love about food is that it brings me back from overwhelming disasters and abstract questions. The forces of the universe sometimes line up in the pecan pie or the pasta. They become not only concrete and tangible; they are also succulent! My broader question, and the purpose of this book, is this: How can we learn to eat in a way that will be deeply satisfying?

I invite you to come along and consider the following rule of life: Christian food practices offer a potent way of teaching us how we might live truly satisfying lives. How to eat well, how to genuinely enjoy, and how to share life to its fullest—all these are by-products of those practices.

Thus, in chapter 1 I look at the eating habits, both healthy and unhealthy, that we have already inevitably adopted. Those habits, once consciously adopted, become practices. Our purpose is to encourage those that are healthy and enjoyable. Toward that end, each subsequent chapter considers an everyday aspect of eating that evokes certain life-shaping practices. The first practice grows out of gratitude, saying grace before meals (chapter 2). We also eat together in community and offer hospitality to others (chapter 3). The practice of feasting, a public celebration of gratitude and joy, draws on the two elements embedded in saying grace and hospitality (chapter 4). Chapter 5 considers a practice that is often forgotten, that of preparing food and cooking. The next two practices—fasting and honoring our bodies—build on self-awareness and confession and evoke self-conscious intentions toward eating. Fasting expresses a desire to deepen one's self-conscious spirituality of eating (chapter 6). Honoring the body moves into the practice of diet and healthy living (chapter 7). Every one of these chapters concludes with a section designed to help us refine and deepen the eating practice described in it, that is, to learn how to eat well. In that way it will point to wise (and practical) ways to encounter God in our daily life.

Chapter 8 draws on all the everyday elements that form the basis of these practices and indicates how they are incorporated into the master practice or sacrament of the Lord's Supper. The Eucharist witnesses to God's life for us and reinforces those practices in us.

Chapter 9 considers the ways in which these healthy practices can become incorporated in the church. They can contribute to building communities of delight and sharing with joy. We will see that the way of giving is the way of receiving and that both giving and receiving are essential to community.

What is set before us in this book is a way of practicing our eating that will fill our souls and our cups to overflowing. I crave for you as I do for myself what God wishes for us: a sense of being fully used, of sharing, and of great delight! *Ṣaddîq* and *shalom*!

ONE

Practicing Eating

"PRACTICE EATING" IS AN ABSURD TITLE, I know. But my point here is simply to indicate that we all develop eating practices that become habits—good, bad, neutral. Some of those habits have to do with the way we were brought up. They became hardwired into our biology. Our biology, however, is not impenetrable to the cultural meanings and stories that we ingest with our food. We are influenced by our important and real biological limits, but we are not trapped like mice into the limits of our protoplasm. We develop stories and meanings that make sense of biology and culture and beliefs. We *can* change our habits. Leon Kass contrasts fueling with dining, an extreme distinction but one that makes the point that we are both biological in our eating (fueling) but also social and cultural (dining).[1]

What I most want to indicate in this chapter is that, although we do develop habits through the way we grow up, we are not determined by them. Even early in our lives we are impacted by both biological and social forces. We have the possibility of changing our script; we are able to take on new narratives, and with them new practices. (Practices are habits we consciously affirm and adopt.) If that sounds as though we are subject to two forces, you are correct. Sometimes we act from force of habit. Some days, I wind up in front of the refrigerator just looking to "see what's there." When I saw my oldest son, Michael, open the refrigerator and just check it out, I realized that there I was. A mirror image experience!

We all have eating habits. Some, like my refrigerator jaunts, are almost unconscious. I used to say that we don't think about food much. But that is clearly untrue. We often think about food as well as operate by force of habit, but we tend to discount our food habits. I think that I ought to be able to control my eating and sometimes think that food just isn't all that important. Maybe it is that food doesn't seem worthy of entering into my life narratives. I often don't think of my food habits or practices as particularly religious, much less Christian. Does this mean that there are sectors of our lives that are too mundane to be open to the influence of faith? Does God care about our bodies, our eating habits? Certainly God cares, I would say. Is that one way that God tries to get in touch with us? I think so. This book is all about changing our narratives and practices so that we can live more abundantly.

We in the United States and other media-saturated nations are so bombarded by food advertisements that we have learned to suppress them. Perhaps, indeed, that is the purpose of advertising—to get us to discount our food experiences except as occasions for fueling up. We are aware of nutrition, but basically we do not see eating and eating practices as the spiritually significant activities they are. As we change our narratives, we also change our practices. For example, if our narrative incorporates a view of ourselves as creatures in an eco-logical web, that will change our practices. Conversely, as we change our practices, we take on different narratives. For example, if our practices are vegetarian, then we might take on a more ecological narrative. The two are symbiotic. Our bodies are an indicator of how satisfactory the narratives we are living out, and the practices they embody, are.

So, in this chapter, I demonstrate how it is that we develop eating practices, why they are significant, and how they can be an avenue to the presence of God. Our bodies are storied; they are narratives that tell part of our stories. But they are *our* bodies, and the narratives they live out are shaped by the practices we engage in.

Prenatal and Infancy Patterns

Our very earliest experiences, even before we were released from our mothers' wombs, were of eating. At that point, the eating was involuntary, beyond our wills or even desires (though we can't be sure about our desires). We just ate. Our earliest postwomb experiences also included eating, and apparently those experiences were quite formative. Although we cannot consciously remember that concentrated, exuberant sucking, perhaps we can imagine the way our bodies may have unconsciously and with total abandon given themselves over to such engrossing satisfaction. There's a visceral edge to that, a residue of good feeling. I wonder just how primal that early learning was, how it lodged itself in our bodies, and how it influenced and continues to impact our lives. How we were fed during our early months of life and into the next year certainly shaped our sense of the goodness of life.

Sometimes even the most alert and appreciative of us forget that eating is a primal delight. We don't have time, we say, to really enjoy our meal. In this book I encourage you to become aware of the way you eat now and to make that experience deeper. In short, I aim to make you alert to all that you do when you eat and open you to the wonder of this everyday event. What we make of our early biological experience enters into our lives, but we are not simply programmed by our early experience, whatever it was. (I hope that yours was delightful, however.)

For babies, breastfeeding has nutritional and health benefits.[2] For mothers who breastfeed, the activity can be an opportunity to bond with their newborns. Cuddling a baby skin to skin while feeding must be immensely satisfying. (I am a bit jealous.) Furthermore, there are health benefits for nursing mothers: a lower risk of breast and ovarian cancers and a reduced risk of osteoporosis, among others.

Alongside the nutrition the infant enjoys, there are other emotional and perhaps even spiritual dispositions or orientations that the infant ingests. Erik Erikson speaks of this first stage in the life of a person as involving the basic psychological conflict of trust versus distrust.[3] Is life trustworthy or not? Can we be confident that the forces of the universe, as manifested here, will be benevolent, or will we find them malevolent and suspicious? Are they open to our shaping, or will they only shape us? Is life a happy adventure or a daily struggle to eke out subsistence? What happens during this basic conflict enters into the way we approach reality.

To add another layer to this, however, consider the fact of generational differences in the accepted wisdom of the moment about breastfeeding. An earlier generation was persuaded that breastfeeding was not the best method of child raising. Perhaps that other generation was right and the accepted wisdom will change again. This brings the ambiguity of both the biology and the cultural norms connected with eating and child raising into view. We operate by the narratives we inherit, by those we choose, and by a dynamic combination of the two.

All is not narrative and choice, however. Imagine that you were born as the child of Congolese parents trapped in a civil and tribal war in the northeastern province of your country. Food is scarce, and the level of terror that comes with confusion about who the fighters are and how to protect oneself surely enter into a mother's capacity for lactation. The level of anxiety that this mother experiences goes far beyond simple ambiguity. In fact, this mother's infant will be fortunate indeed if his or her mother gets enough to eat to produce breast milk in sufficient quantity to nourish her child. This child's life chances are not promising, to understate the case. Could this child grow up experiencing the world as trustworthy? It is difficult to imagine.

The contrast between an affluent American mother and the indigent Congolese mother makes us aware of just how many of our life opportunities get expressed in the quality of the food we eat and the situation in which we eat it. The food we eat and our ability to eat it in relative safety and security express our living conditions. It would be an overstatement to say that all life comes down to eating, but it is clear that our eating reflects our life situation. We are not only *what* we eat; we are also *how* we eat. And what begins in infancy as a reflection of our parents' beliefs, values, and socioeconomic situation tends to continue to be embodied in the ways we eat and how we experience food. Food is so embedded in our everyday experience that we can easily remain unconscious about the beliefs, values, and practices in which we are engaged. We are largely oblivious to our food patterns because they are so much with us. Much about our eating is involuntary; for example, we attend very little to the whole process of digestion. Equally involuntary are our very earliest experiences. Furthermore, in our busyness we tend not to devote too much thought to eating even now. We simply do it. Most of us grow up with both good and bad habits and practices of eating. Thus it becomes significant to reflect on our eating habits. What are we doing? What do we express by the way we eat?

Early Childhood Eating Habits

As our experiences of eating accumulate, we realize that our eating falls into certain patterns and eventually forms a set of habits. We eat a hearty breakfast while others are satisfied with a glass of milk. We feel we *have* to eat at lunchtime while others often find they have forgotten lunch altogether. Some people, like the Congolese child, may not have a consistent schedule for eating.

One reason so many people get exercised about the impact of food advertising on television, especially on Saturday morning, is that a great many young kids watch those ads. Long before they can discern the hype from the real, their eating practices are being shaped. Do you wonder why all the national reports on obesity include the percentage of young children in that category? I suspect it is because we bemoan the fact that young children do not yet have the full capacity to choose what they will eat, how often they will eat, and how much physical activity they will be permitted. They simply are not yet fully responsible. We therefore blame their parents and their upbringing to some extent. Greg Critser, in his book *Fat Land: How Americans Became the Fattest People in the World*,[4] relates that many children exhibit the onset of early diabetes (type 2 diabetes), a disease that is associated with childhood obesity. This is also a problem for adults, of course.

I remember that, as a child, I became quite conscious of the fact that I was both taller and husky (a nice word) than other boys my age. Already a narrative about my body was developing internally, and that narrative was ambiguous. Not only was I bigger, but I was seeking to explore the meaning of being bigger. One part of this narrative was that I was not very good at sports.

Early childhood eating practices set the stage for later ones. The pattern of eating in front of the television helps make us unaware of what our bodies are telling us. This is a habit that contributes to our not attending to the messages our bodies are sending us. We eat haphazardly, often because we are simply restless or distracted. (This is sounding increasingly autobiographical, gentle reader. Are you with me?)

Our parents may have encouraged us to get out of the house and exercise. They may have expressed a positive attitude about playing outside, and they may have played with us or arranged for us to participate in sports or some other outdoor activity. They may have encouraged good patterns of eating. In many ways, our parents, our location of birth, and the people around us as we were growing up influenced us a great deal toward healthy or less-than-healthy practices of eating. We became more or less conscious of what and how we were eating. With increasing consciousness, we began to reflect on our habits, and they began to develop into practices.

Food as Interpersonal

The important pattern of eating with others develops early. Eating is primordially a social act shared by parents and child. Eating together is a sign of our common humanity; maybe it is a family pattern passed on from family to family. Whatever the reasons, eating together seems inexorably a social practice. We don't like to eat alone. We enjoy eating with others, sharing stories and the day's events, or simply being together. This pattern has a long history. In some countries that tradition of eating together is breaking down, which is a cause for alarm. For most people there still appears to be something that links eating with being together socially and sharing a meal.

What did you (and I, for that matter) learn about sharing? Was it polite to eat in front of other people without sharing? The voice of my mother resonates in my skull even yet. We were supposed to share, at least when there were other people present. We also learned to share from the earliest days of being in church. There was a sense that, if you had enough yourself, you were supposed to share with those who were "less fortunate"—maybe that Congolese child.

A final childhood experience is whether or not we knew where the food came from. Did your family have a garden? Did your church or school or your grandparents have one? Were there flowers in your yard? Maybe you were expected to do some weeding or to pick the tomatoes or raspberries. The pattern of knowing where your food came from probably fed into an appreciation for fresh food and also for the garden plot that nourished the food. Maybe it even contributed to a budding appreciation for planetary health. Your church may have encouraged an appreciation of plants and animals. At the height of the growing season, many people share tomatoes or cucumbers or zucchini or other vegetables with others. Many churches have food pantries or a "deacon's fund" to assist those who are hungry. Your story may have included the experience of picking tomatoes or raspberries, or maybe it involved buying them from the store. At this point there was some bodily knowledge (or not) that became a part of your story (or not). The line between bodily knowledge and cultural knowledge seems quite thin at this nexus.

Economic Insights

As we get older we learn to equate food with money. Maybe we went grocery shopping and our Mom or Dad taught us to check out bargains or to compare brands of cereals for cost. Maybe our parent noted the price of raspberries in December and remarked, "Wow, would you look at that! Who could afford to buy those?" Or maybe we had allowances and found that we couldn't get the huge sack of Reese's Pieces that we wanted. Or maybe when we went out to eat, our parents wouldn't let us order the lobster at what was called "market price," and they explained in dollars and cents.

At any rate, we began to get conflicting understandings about food. Our narratives became even more complex. If we had learned something about where food comes from as a result of gardening in the backyard, and then had one of these economic experiences, we began to learn to equate food with consumer costs as well. When money narratives entered our story, food became somewhat more distanced from who we were.

At school, kids see vending machines, and they also find familiar brands in the lunch line. They begin to calculate how much money they have left and where to spend it. Our children get sophisticated and savvy about the cost of food and about how relatively cheap it is. Food is easily available everywhere without great cost. We begin to equate economic cost with the value of food.

Indeed, as with many "consumer goods," we begin to associate food with money. Food begins to seem like an additional item in the family budget, and the process of commodification is well under way before we become fully cognizant of it. We consider virtuous those who "manage their money well," shop for bargains, live without unnecessary debt, and are frugal and careful about money. "Finding a bargain" comes close to being a civic virtue in the United States. Some, by contrast, claim that we have become *homo economicus*[5] (the economic human), reducing the value of everything to quantitative, monetary terms and equating the value of material goods with their price. Food, however, cannot finally be reduced to monetary cost, because food is essential to life. Furthermore, the quality and quantity of food available to us determines our opportunities in life.

Nowhere and at no time on our planet has food ever been as inexpensive as it is now in the United States, at least when we consider the average percentage of income that people spend on food. Food is to be cheap, available, and easily accessible. Because of this we sometimes fail to appreciate the value of food as a category of public policy. Furthermore, a great deal of effort goes into encouraging us toward the overconsumption of food.[6]

Economically, it may be that the root of many of our food patterns is that we have too much and consume too much, and that food is too cheap. It makes us forget what food is; it becomes difficult to imagine that there are people both in this country and in many countries in the world who do not have enough. Where food is scarce, people consume too little and food is too dear. The problem is the unjust distribution of food; the food supply system is stacked in favor of a small minority and against the majority. Those of us who have too much have simply forgotten what food is or how significant it is.

Environmental Practices

When food becomes equated with dollars and cents, we forget that it is a natural product grown by people who work the soil. If we are to eat healthy food, we need to be sure that plants and animals are grown carefully in a sustainable way. This makes gardening, whether vegetables or flowers, an important practice. It reminds us that the tomato we eat is an environmental product—and so are we. Similarly, if we raise chickens or cows, we are reminded of the interdependence of life.

Gardening or raising livestock makes us conscious of the work that goes into raising plants and animals. We become—at least briefly—farmers, and we become conscious that our actions have environmental consequences and that growing food requires effort. (Our family probably had the most labor-intensive tomatoes and cilantro in Dubuque, Iowa!) Farming is work, and work is an activity that is part of the ecological web. We recognize the integral connections between food, nature, and work by a wide range of practices. We say grace before meals. We recognize the cooks and wait staff after a meal by tipping or calling the staff out to be applauded. We go to the farmers market. We are attentive to where food comes from. It is easy to lose these connections in a society where our work, the food industry, and environmental well-being seem like separate sectors.

I could continue this catalog. Indeed, food practices are involved in many other aspects of our lives, such as practicing hospitality and welcoming others, respecting and enjoying our bodies, and shaping the strength of community by eating together. Many rituals of bonding center around shared meals.[7] Some have said that one can determine the health of a church by the quality of its potlucks! However exaggerated that may be, there is a kernel of truth there. It seems easier to listen to each other attentively and to talk at some depth when eating together. The community thus formed can strengthen our resistance to destructive forces.[8] Sharing meals with others strengthens our resolve to share life-giving patterns with those who are hungry for food, spiritual depth, and soul food.

Mindlessness and Becoming Mindful

Eating is not a magical process. There are probably as many negative patterns or practices accompanying eating as there are positive ones. What makes the difference between eating as a life-giving, community-binding, healthy practice and one that is destructive, fragmenting, and illness-producing? One factor is simple mindlessness, not paying attention to what food is or to the ways we eat and the consequences of our practices.

This may seem to be a shallow, if not a naïve point. However, sin and evil accompany such mindlessness, and mindlessness can be seen as related to original sin. We may remain "intentionally" mind*less* when being mind*ful* threatens our self-interest. Indeed, the events that led to the oppression of the Jewish people in the 1930s and 1940s or to South African apartheid or to "ethnic cleansing" in recent decades involved the momentum of mindlessness. By not paying attention, or by paying only selective attention, we allow the forces of evil to go unchecked. We may fail to resist because we intuit that to do so might be uncomfortable, difficult, or dangerous. Marilyn Frye makes a distinction between the "arrogant eye" and the "loving eye" that enters into the way we approach any project or person, a distinction that suggests just how open we will be to learning or relating.[9] There may also be a lazy or indifferent eye that fails to explore the consequences of contemporary practices or patterns of action.

Our food practices are shaped by large corporate and societal forces. We do not intentionally *choose* our eating practices at first so much as we are inculcated into them. We can become mindless by following cultural norms. We can be inculcated into destructive and narcotizing habits and also into habits that are healthy and grace-filled. But we need not simply follow our visceral reactions as though social training were destiny. We have the capacity to become aware of and to reflect on our habits and patterns. We can choose to follow practices that communicate the grace of God to others and to ourselves. We can become mindful.

As Stephanie Paulsell writes, "Without practices that help us seek God's presence in the ordinary moments of our lives, we will miss countless opportunities to draw near to the God who made us."[10] Put positively, practices help us seek God's presence and actively pursue those that are most fertile for human flourishing. Clearly this is not automatic; we have to train ourselves. We have to practice! We may not choose the activities and practices that are best for us, which God would choose for us. We trust our own choices, even though we know that those can turn out disastrously. The disciplines of spiritual study and reflection can be of immense assistance in combating the forces of sin and evil. Historical practices are still proving themselves capable of building Christian character; they are great body- and community-building exercises as well.

God is alive and present in our lives, in the life of the church, and in the life of the culture. Christians proclaim that food is a good gift of God, as are our bodies. Both Hebrew Scripture and the New Testament reveal the purposes for which God intends food to be used: for engendering delight and encouraging sharing. Certain practices promote delight and sharing while others lead to despair and hoarding. Through the power of the Spirit, we seek to practice those activities that make for life in ourselves and others, and also to resist those that destroy the goodness of our lives and permit violence, starvation, and sickness to ravage the lives of others. Food practices are one of God's ways of encouraging life, of resisting sin and evil, and of building community.

The purpose of this book is to identify practices that make for delight and sharing, practices that please God and build community. I have already pointed to several areas of life where God is working to foster health:

- the ways we eat (diet and exercise)
- the sharing of food in community
- feasting and fasting (the economics of food)
- a respect for nature (both human and nonhuman)
- food practices in the life of the local church

There is a master model that can inform all the food practices I consider here. That master model is the sacrament of the Eucharist or the Lord's Supper. Virtually every Christian church recognizes Jesus' institution of this food practice as one of its sacraments, a visible and tangible sign of an invisible and intangible grace. The Lord's Supper is a particularly rich expression of the activity and truth of God, a place where God is especially present. The thick levels of meaning embedded in the sacrament have much to teach us, as they contain many Christian beliefs embedded in a concrete, tangible, and efficacious sign. But, before I take up the Eucharist as a model, I want to identify tangible ways to experience God's presence in our everyday food practices. The Eucharist is such a powerful symbol that it can not only reveal but also obscure the everyday practices that God moves through. It can foster the notion that every instance of eating is Christian and thus, ironically, disguise the way God is present. The life of the Spirit works through the world and not only through the church and Christian sacraments.

Thinking about Our Practices

I conclude each chapter with a section designed to further your own reflection on eating practices. In order to encourage and include the learning styles of a variety of participants, these questions and actions will stimulate you to connect your ideas and feelings to the content of each chapter.

1. In the introduction to this book, I pointed out that the Swahili word *ubuntu* expresses the idea that one's own well-being is increased by the well-being of others. In considering this concept in terms of eating, how has your well-being been enhanced by others in the past month at home or at social gatherings? Does knowing the word *ubuntu* help to make the experience more meaningful? If so, how? Think about the idea, and then share your thoughts with someone close to you.

2. Make a brief list of the various stages of your life: infancy, pre-school, elementary age, teen years, young adult, middle age, and elder years (whatever stage you have reached). Pick one or two stages and identify an experience that was enriched by the sharing of food. How is the memory more intense because food was involved?

3. Discuss the list you made in item two with someone else and see what you can add to yours. What things had you forgotten or remembered as being significant, or remembered differently? What did the quality and kind of food have to do with the experience? How does the experience differ with the age and gender of the persons? Decide on some different ways of planning similar activities.

4. Before continuing to the next chapter, examine your daily eating experiences. Which are shared? Are they better or less satisfying when other people are involved? What one change could you make to enhance your eating experience tomorrow? Rather than planning diet menus for the week, try planning life-changing eating experiences for the week, including different people and different foods.

TWO

Saying Grace at the Labna

AN ANCIENT MAYAN CITY NAMED LABNA once stood on the Yucatan Peninsula of Mexico. My wife, Patti, and I love the peninsula—Cancun, Chichen-Itza (Mayan ruins), snorkeling, the beach, the sun. But maybe, just maybe, the best parts are the *restaurante*.

The owners of La Habichuela (one of our favorites) have created another marvelous restaurant called Labna, named after the Mayan city. As you approach, you realize the architecture outside resembles one of the pyramid burial tombs. It is layered like stairs. Inside, the same layering has been used on the ceiling and covered with burlap to resemble being inside the pyramid. On one wall is a mural of the Mayan city, framed by an entanglement of tropical vines and trees. There are banana and palm trees inside as well.

Living up to the beauty of the place, the *sopa de lima* (chicken soup with lime) is just flat-out unbelievable. The waiter, Aidrian, brought us bowls of tortilla strips and chicken meat topped with slices of lime. Then he filled a soup ladle with chicken-lime soup and covered the tortilla-lime-chicken. Who would have thought such a conglomeration would taste so wonderful? It almost changed my idea of what soup is! It was a good thing we said grace first.

Patti's entrée was the *Labna Especial*, a grilled strip of pork marinated in lime, sour Yucatan orange, chili/tomato sauce, and served with traditional sausage, tortillas stuffed with boiled eggs bathed in pumpkin and green sauce, and black beans on the side. I had the *Cochinita Pibil*, tender pork seasoned with acriote, wrapped in banana leaves and baked in a slow oven. Talk about heaven! The Labna pork marinated in lime was outstanding, as was my *cochinita*, which tasted like the best barbeque I've ever had, with just a touch of sweetness.

We have to go back to Cancun for their dessert—and the suckling pig with guacamole sauce, and maybe their flamed strawberries. Hey, sometimes you just have to suffer.

Eating is not something we have to force ourselves to do. Most of us enjoy eating and even look forward to it. In many ways it structures our days; we plan to do certain things over lunch with friends or business acquaintances; we plan a family time at supper. Things go better with lunch. Or supper. Or breakfast.

My friend Tom says that he doesn't really like to eat. Where we go for lunch doesn't matter to him; it's all the same. I never did understand that. I still don't. In fact, I so much fail to understand it that I don't believe it. If I did believe it, then I would have to pity Tom for lacking the gift of enjoying eating. I love eating. And I believe most people do.

To be sure, food sustains life itself. It is not just another product, not just a commodity. Providing food to others is a gospel imperative; growing and distributing food is far more than a policy or vocational choice. A bumper sticker says, "If you eat, thank a farmer." It is a way of feeding the next-door neighbor but also the world, as any farmer will tell you; it is not just an economic choice. It is a joy, a joy that explains what keeps some farmers growing food after years of just breaking even.

Food and those who grow it touch all our lives, wherever we live. We depend on those who plant the seed, cultivate, combine, and harvest. We depend on those communities and companies who support agriculture and growers' families and those who package, transport, and sell food.

But those who grow very little of their own food think differently about food than those who do or those who don't have enough. Most North Americans do think about the quality of the food that we have. And, even though our food security is sometimes threatened—witness the mad cow scare of spring 2004—by and large we have great food in the United States.

As essential as eating is, for the secure North American, European, or East Asian, this dependency barely crosses our anxiety threshold—if at all. For us middle- and upper-income people (surely upper income by the globe's standards), we simply assume there will be enough high-quality food, and we have become largely unconscious of what food is. Indeed, at base we are absolutely dependent as human animals upon food—no doubt about it. However, the availability of food is so deeply assumed that famine no longer registers as a threat. And for that we say, "Praise the Lord."

Our response to the bounty that we have received is gratitude and joy. At least, one would think that the level of material comfort and well-being that most of us enjoy in the United States would generate that sort of response. And, frankly, it often does. My question is why we don't seem to enjoy eating (and the rest of our lives) more. I explored that in an earlier book and basically concluded that we have so much and have been so blessed that we have fallen into the disorder of excess. A little self-imposed scarcity might increase our enjoyment. There is such a thing as "too much" that dampens both the delight we take in eating and also our ability to share, both of which are close to what it means to be human. Delight and sharing are two of the purposes for which God created food and humankind.

This chapter will locate the basis for the joy and thanksgiving that are a central motivation for the Christian life. The great bounty and goodness that God has given to us and all people summons us to lives of joy and sharing. I describe some of the reasons for the joy that Christians exhibit. I then suggest that the way we shape our food practices also shapes us, others around us, and the present and future health of the planet. Those practices are most significantly a way of opening ourselves to God that results in our own deep happiness. Finally, I look at a practice that expresses that joy and gratitude—saying grace before meals.

Food as a Source of Joy

From the beginning, food has been central to the Christian faith. Not only is food basic to our daily lives, but so are the ways we grow, distribute, and eat food. These things shape our wider economy and politics. Not only are we what we eat, but also we are *how* we eat. The Hebrew people knew that, and some of their hymns of praise express the basic faith that it is Yahweh, the God and Father of our Lord Jesus Christ, who creates and gives us food. It is God who sends rain "on the just and on the unjust," as Jesus put it (Matt. 5:45). God is the ultimate source of all life and the means for its sustenance.

Christians and Jews have recognized God as the source of that which gives them much delight: food. This has evoked gratitude and praise. Cathy Campbell suggests that "joy—the heart delighted—is at the very core of discipleship."[1] Since joy is indeed a major component of the Christian life, we can benefit by looking at some of the many ways that God has blessed us through food.

1. The first thing to identify as a source of joy is the *sheer goodness* of food. Yes, I know, food is essential. What never ceases to amaze me is just how responsive my body is to food. You set a rack of lamb in front of me and I am ready to go! Did you experience my salivating at the Labna when I described the *Cochinita Pibil?* Food is so much more engaging than it would need to be if it were only about sustaining life. (For good reason, the full-meal-in-a-pill schemes will never catch on!) God made food appetizing—not only nutritious.

There are two things about the goodness of food that clamor for notice. One is the *involuntary* nature of our bodily reactions. We have been created in such a way that our bodily facilities are activated by food in socially as well as physically constructed ways. This response links the quality of our food to our embodiment. The repulsion we may feel at the sight or smell of some foods (for example, eating crab cold and raw, a South Korean delicacy) simply reinforces the involuntary quality of the body's response that I'm highlighting. On the other hand, the smell of pecan pie is enticing to me—but just as involuntary.

The other is the *mystery* of the connection, the relationship between our bodies and food. Somehow our senses have been trained to like certain foods and dislike others. Stewed tomatoes will never be big for me—a fact that I attribute to the cuisine at my elementary school cafeteria in Zachary, Louisiana. In contrast, we may find ourselves ready to devour pictures and descriptions of foods we enjoy. Remember your reaction to the description of the specials by your waiter at a fine restaurant! How and why our bodies and minds are so viscerally engaged by the prospect and experience of eating retains an edge of mystery, but we do know that this is a source of joy!

2. Equally significant as a source of joy is the way that we are in *relationship with the entire earth community*, other human beings and other species as well. As embodied beings, we are dependent on a whole range of "consumables." One of these that we take for granted is a substance that we "ingest," "take in," and "gulp," a substance that "nourishes" and "sustains" us, and one that we cannot do without for five minutes. It is invisible. The substance? Air.

David Abram, in *The Spell of the Sensuous*, reminds us that the activity of breathing—like eating and drinking—destroys the fiction that we can have a pure "interior" being apart from an "exterior" one that is part of the web of life.[2] Abram's point is that there is no escaping our linkage to the earth. Thinking about consuming food and drink makes this case almost as dramatically as does that of our breathing. We inhabit a more-than-human world with which we are integrally related. We deny, repress, or ignore "our thorough interdependence with the other animals, the plants and the living land that sustains us" only at our peril.[3] We are embodied beings who exist in relationship, who are dependent upon the wider earth community. We cannot shed our bodies. Instead, they reveal the extent of our interdependence; our bodies themselves are relational.

Now, as Abram has intimated, we may resist acknowledging and eventually accepting our communal embeddedness. We may not see or feel this embodied dependency as a source of joy at all. Some people do minimize their sense of embodied dependence. But what does it mean to delude ourselves by not acknowledging that dependency—to obscure such an essential part of our being or refuse to take it into account?

At least to some extent we choose to accept our membership in the earth community. We consent to the joys of relating to other human beings—making love, feasting, long conversations, exercising together. We may enjoy the world of animals; gardening, hiking, or kayaking; sunshine and rain; eating and drinking. Though some aspects of our embodied relationality are involuntary and not in dispute, our response to them is at least partially under our influence. Men and women accept a portion of their relationality and recognize it as a source of joy. We can glory in our relationship with the earth community and enjoy all the delights that provides.

3. The third gift that evokes our joy and gratitude is the capacity to exercise *some measure of control* over our lives, including our health and spiritual well-being. Eating is integral to both and will be the focus here.

At least to some extent we can shape the involuntary processes of sensuousness and relationality through our attention to the dimensions of health and spirituality. By being mindful of the food we eat, we can in fact change our attitudes toward eating and possibly our diet as well. We can begin to appreciate all that has gone into getting food on our tables. One example of attitudinal change is the choice of many young people—such as our son Nathan—not to eat red meat or indeed any meat. That choice calls into question my being carnivorous, and it begins to change my attitude. The current discussion of obesity and related health concerns has made us as a society alert to our eating habits as well. There is no doubt that our attitudes about food and eating are changing.

Another area in which we have discretion—although we cannot know for certain the quality or safety of the food we are eating—is the decisions we make in buying different foods. We can grow some of our own food; we can eat organic foods; we can buy locally. We can change our diets by eating foods we know to be healthy, equitably priced, ecologically benign, and nutritionally balanced.

Deborah Kersten hypothesizes that spirituality is the missing ingredient in our food and that we can learn to appreciate this spiritual dimension. In the course of her research on eating in countries that have different religious traditions, she

> came to regard food as a work of art that needs to be appreciated in its totality. For I discovered that in addition to the Hindu belief that espouses approaching food with loving regard, other wisdom traditions encourage us to honor food, and to partake of it with a depth and sincerity that make it sacred. . . . The implication: when we furnish food with such sacred understanding, it will nourish both body and soul in ways we have been depriving ourselves of.[4]

It is hard to know how much this contributes to healthy eating. Nevertheless, we know from experience that how we eat, the setting in which we eat, and how we allow food to enter into our digestive processes makes a difference. (Who has not had a stomachache after wolfing down a Big Mac and fries?) We *can* learn to eat well and enjoyably.

Finally, there has been an explosion of research and policy discussion at the national level concerning how we eat. We saw the food supply system being reshaped by the power of the Atkins and South Beach diets.[5] Indeed, even Pepsi and Coke responded to these trends as low-carb menus became ubiquitous. This is all very encouraging for the health of affluent peoples and suggests that we might learn to delight in eating well. Regaining a sense of physical well-being could contribute to spiritual health as well; we might thereby learn to share with others.[6]

Christians recognize all these sources of joy as having their origin in the Creator; that same God continues to be present creating, redeeming, and sustaining the world; this included all that is involved in our eating. I have pointed to several sources of joy that demonstrate the goodness and providence of God in our eating. Christians respond to God's initiative in Christ and Spirit through worship, praise, and thanksgiving, among other practices.

Saying Grace

One routine, sometimes inconspicuous way we respond to the sources of joy that God provides is by praying before meals. (In the case of Jewish people, often the longer prayer follows the meal. This *berakah* or benediction is described by Thomas Simons.)[7] It is interesting that many of those who have become disaffected or alienated from the church often bow their heads or pause before eating. So powerful is this little practice that it just feels right to acknowledge the source of our food. But this practice is anything but innocuous or simple. There are multiple layers to its meaning and its formative power. I want to tap two of those here. First, I look at three aspects of its *theological* meaning and, second, I turn to some experiential implications for practicing the saying of grace.

Theological Meanings

There are three different ways of labeling such a routine prayer. One "says grace" before meals; another gives a "table blessing"; still another "gives thanks" before eating. For Christians they are all based, of course, on Jesus' blessing of meals (among other examples, see Luke 9:16; 22:17; 24:30; and John 6:11, 23). The Gospel writers saw in Jesus' action the traditional custom of recognizing "the fruits of the field which grew through the power of God's blessing and for which we are to give our humble thanks to the Creator."[8] Thus Jesus' expression of thanks was a recognition of God's having already blessed our daily bread. The three different expressions for the practice of praying before meals point to different features. Linking them is an outpouring of praise and gratitude to God.

- *Saying grace.* The fundamental structure of every blessing is that of glorifying and acknowledging the goodness and might of God. We "say grace" to recognize God's grace. It is fundamentally a worshipful event that names and confesses God as the source of our food, on whom we depend for our lives. To be sure, the gift of food (and especially its smell as we are waiting) evokes a small eruption of praise, homage, and thanks. But it is first of all not an entreaty to God but a doxological (praising) event.[9]

- *Table blessing.* The Gospels frequently use the formula, "looked up to heaven, blessed and broke the bread" (Matt. 14:19; Mark 6:14; Luke 9:16; 24:30). Here Jesus is blessing God, as the customary Jewish host would have done. We are thereby commended to return blessings back to the heavenly source of our blessing. Blessing from above calls for our blessing from below. John Koenig suggests that "we can hardly doubt that Jesus' earliest followers found his blessings over food to be materially transforming."[10] There is a missional thrust here. Koenig seems to be implying that as we bless God, we are transformed. As we render blessing back to the Great Source of Blessing, we are ourselves blessed by the food, the bread and wine God gives. We are to practice in accord with the Spirit of God's action, to bless as we are blessed, to share as God has shared. And so we pray, "Bless this food to our use, and us in your service," or an equivalent phrase.

- *Giving thanks.* The outpouring of gratitude is interrelated and in fact undergirds the other emphases. Often this giving thanks is linked to a request for continued provision. The petition in the Lord's Prayer, "Give us this day our daily bread" (Matt. 6:11; or "every day," Luke 11:3), is especially instructive. Koenig suggests that in this petition Jesus was alluding to the way God sent manna in the wilderness (enough only for each day) and also linking this petition to the former one,

"Your kingdom come on earth as in heaven." The Greek word translated "this day" (*epiousious*) seems close to "supersubstantial" rather than to "daily."[11] Jesus probably had the great banquet or feast of the Great Tomorrow in mind and was suggesting that our eating could be a transcendent event, "a foretaste of the feast to come." "To ask that God's joyous abundance might come to us" this day suggests that it is here "within the everyday gatherings of his disciples."[12] We get a glimpse of it even as we are giving thanks and asking God for continued providence. Thus the way we eat—in dependence on God and in anticipation of the full reign of God—expresses gratitude and carries through in our living. We are to eat here ("on earth") as though we were eating in heaven. Sometimes we even get a taste of that! We feel that *jouissance* that goes beyond the taste of the food as we sense ourselves linked to the wider creation, for example, at Eucharist (see Matt. 26:27; Mark 14:23; Luke 22:17–19; 1 Cor. 11:23). Thus the eschatological dimension is joined to the material in our simple table graces.

Experiential Implications

Wherein lies the power of the experience of saying grace? That is the practical issue I want to raise. There are two groups of participants to consider: adults and children.

For adults, the experience of saying grace is powerful because it communicates the theological meanings mentioned above. It does this in ways that connect the everyday, practical, holistic sense of lived experience with the transcendent source of the practice—Jesus. Thus the theological meaning of saying grace can be described in terms of behavior or practices.

The experience itself has power in that when we say grace we acknowledge our dependence on a power beyond ourselves. In effect, we bow our heads in order to honor and praise God. Frequently we feel the Spirit there in a way that we seldom do otherwise. While I don't think we always experience this formative effect with the same immediacy, over time our attitudes and character are shaped by the practice of saying grace. We are formed spiritually and morally by this routine prayer. At the very times when we say grace, we may be closest to being hungry. Monika Hellwig suggests, "To be hungry is to experience oneself as insufficient, as having needs, as being unable to guarantee one's own existence."[13] Thus perhaps we discover in saying grace an impulse to surrender control, to trust, to be dependent. And that may feel good!

This brings us to consider the experience of children. In my family of origin, saying grace was a practice that was almost as natural as eating itself. I very seldom even thought about it, much less reflected on the praises and petitions we spoke. I went through a phase where I was too embarrassed to say grace in public and have now become a militant grace-sayer in public restaurants. There are a lot of meals to be blessed in a restaurant.

Saying grace is terrifically important for children. Most significantly, being formed in gratitude as a response to grace may be the foundation of living faithfully and joyously. "Gratitude," writes John Mogabgab, "gathers us in that double helix of grace descending and praise ascending that forms the basic design of life with God." It is "the gesture of a heart opened to receive God"; it "refreshes our minds with the memory of God's gracious way."[14] It reminds children that they can go into the future with trust and assurance in the goodness of God.

Sometimes parents have difficulty in transporting the activities of the faith from the sanctuary to the kitchen. Children seem to be learning less and less about anything religious at home. We should see the home and family as sacred and as immediate and profound contexts for spiritual learning. Surely practicing the saying of grace is one formative way of learning who we are. It also enables us to pay attention as a spiritual discipline.

Children's saying grace is also instructive for their parents. Michael Williams has a great, almost archetypal story about his two-year-old daughter, Sarah, one night putting her hands together and surprising her parents with a "Thank you food." Later in the meal it was "Thank you Mommy. Thank you Daddy. Thank you Spankie" (their cat).[15] Williams picks up from this epiphany the characteristics of simplicity, spontaneity, and unrestrained desire. Thus "to say grace is to respond to God's gracious gifts simply and spontaneously and with unrestrained delight. . . . To say grace with our voices and our lives is to join hands with others in a community that expresses . . . delight in one another and the creation."[16] Thus parents learn to reexperience delight and joy.

Learning to Say Grace

I turn now to the concrete matter of how to learn to say grace. This section might seem elementary to those of you for whom saying grace before meals is a routine practice. And apparently most Americans do. A 1997 Gallup poll reported that 63 percent of Americans gave a table blessing before meals, up from 47 percent in 1947.[17]

However, if you are like me, you don't think much about this. So the intent of this section is to stimulate you into thinking about what saying grace is and to offer some ways of saying grace. I conclude by asking some questions and providing examples for your reflection and discussion with others.

First, we need to ask ourselves what it is we are doing when we say grace before meals. Most simply, we are giving thanks to God for the food God has provided. (In the Small Catechism, Martin Luther maintained that when we say in the Lord's Prayer, "Give us this day our daily bread," we are in effect thanking God for all our possessions.) We are expressing our gratitude to God for all the ways the world is arranged so as to bring food and sustenance to our table. Suggestion: If you are eating by yourself, you may want to think about what you are doing; if you are eating with others, you may want to discuss this with them. What is this thing we do?

Second, let us wait a bit before we eat. Let's take five seconds or so and just stop. That five seconds may be the best time we spend today.

We can pause after we put the food on the table or before we serve ourselves. Slow down. Before we devour our food, let us think just a moment about what we are doing. Smell the food, look at it, alert our senses to what this is. We might think about what it took to get this to the table.

A Scottish table grace puts it well:

> No ordinary meal—a sacrament awaits us
> On our table daily spread.
> For men are risking lives on sea and land
> That we may dwell in safety and be fed.[18]

Third, let's bow our heads. We needn't touch the floor, but just sit down and bow our heads a bit. This will establish the posture of humility and gratitude for the food whose origins are so far beyond your and my ability to imagine. Remember that it is God whom we are thanking, but also that God uses intermediaries, like the earth and sunshine and farmers and grocery stores.

Fourth, if we are eating with others, let us say our grace aloud. (Some examples will follow, but there are many good books of table blessings; check amazon.com or barnesandnoble.com.) I like to hold hands with those around the table. This reminds me and them that we are in fellowship with each other. It also can enable those gathered to cut through—at least a bit—tension that exists among members.

Fifth, there are different parts of the prayer. I put an asterisk by those that are most important.

★Address: Dear Lord, Almighty God, Gracious Creator.
★Thanksgiving: Thank you for this food.
    Mention of specific foods or people involved in the meal.
    Recognition of passing on the blessings provided.
★Amen.

Here we have, in a very simple form, the three elements of recognizing the origin of our food, an indication of the blessings we have received, the impulse to pass those blessings on, and an expression of gratitude.

Sixth, during the meal itself and especially at its beginning, try to savor the food and continue to give thanks by enjoying the meal. I am a big fan of the "Slow Food" movement, because I think that it is calling us to a greater appreciation of ourselves and our lives. It commends local, fresh, and healthy foods and drink that we can all open ourselves to enjoy.[19]

Questions for Reflection and Action

1. Which of the preceding six points do you disagree with? (Disagreeing is a good way to grow.) Select one and prepare a two-minute defense of your position. Share it with the group of readers.

2. After you consider the template for constructing a grace (in the description of the fifth point above), create a grace. Next, see if your grace could fit a well-known tune, such as "Twinkle, Twinkle, Little Star," "Baa, Baa, Black Sheep," or another. Teach that grace to those at the table. (Maybe it would be good to do this before the cook sets the meal on the table.) Everyone could be taught the new blessing and it could be sung. How does singing together affect the experience?

   A further variation could be to have all persons write their own grace and go around the table saying, rather than singing, it. They should be short. How does multiple grace affect the experience?

3. Almost everyone uses words to say grace. Even singing still uses words. Can you imagine other ways to express a wordless grace? Sign language, pictures, and charades are just a few examples. Try it to examine how the experience changes.

4. Does saying grace make food taste better? How does checking in with God before eating change your religious and gustatory experience?

5. Experiment with your family or those you eat with frequently, changing the positioning of the grace from the beginning to some other location in the meal. Is it better at the end? Does stopping at the middle for grace make you more thankful? More appreciative of the food?

Here are some favorite table graces. You may want to find one and try it out, or you may want to customize your own. It may be interesting to look at them to discover in them the different elements I described above.

> God is great!
> God is good!
> Let us thank God
> For our food.
> Amen.

> Be present at our table, Lord.
> Be here and everywhere adored,
> Thy mercies bless, and grant that we
> May strengthened for thy service be.

> Oh, the Lord's been good to us,
> And so we thank the Lord,
> For giving us the things we need,
> The sun and the rain and the apple seed.

For every seed we sow,
Another tree will grow,
And soon there'll be an orchard there,
For everyone in the world to share.

Come, Lord Jesus
Be our guest
And let these gifts
To us be blest!

Blest be God
Who is our bread!
Let all the world
Be clothed and fed!

I like the little book edited by McElwain (see note 18), which has prayers from various religious traditions and countries. Best of all are the prayers one formulates on the spot.

A final note: The full impact of praying before meals is not clear to me. I believe, though, that its impact is vastly underestimated. It is not just a rote thing we do. But even if it is totally automatic, the practice of saying grace is important. If nothing else, it preserves the form of asking God's blessing. Just because it feels routine doesn't mean that it is viscerally trivial. The expression of gratitude is spiritually formative. Such rituals and traditions shape us.

THREE

Sharing and Hospitality: The Basic Christian Practice?

"YOU DON'T KNOW WHAT YOU'VE GOT TILL IT'S GONE." Or, we might say, some things become prominent by their absence.

Thus it was in Lamont, Iowa. The good citizens and church members of Lamont had lost the last café in their town. Mabel and Sam had decided they were just too old to carry on, and no one was interested in buying their place. The café was where the townspeople, local farmers, and anybody else in town got together in the morning to have a cup of coffee and maybe a doughnut and shoot the breeze. Most heavy decisions got made there. Lunch was when you could count on some of the older townspeople and maybe some others coming in to get a bite to eat. Supper was sometimes heavy, sometimes light. But the fact remained that the last café in Lamont had closed. The only other place to be served something to eat without going out of town was the tavern. Now taverns come in all stripes and dispositions, but this one was not a community sort of place. People felt uncomfortable going into the tavern to eat.

What had become evident to the good people of Lamont was that they needed a place to share a meal, share their news, and build community. The need for such a place had become evident through its absence. I am happy to report that the churches, with the help of an inventive and outgoing United Methodist pastor, got together and decided to open such a place. It is called Common Grounds, and it is a simple coffee-and-sandwiches café—nothing very complicated, but it is volunteer rich, has strong grassroots support, and is a place for community building. On Sunday mornings the high school groups of all the churches gather there. Throughout the week members of the community gather for breakfast, coffee, and other meals. Opening this café impressed me. It wasn't too hard to do, but it took initiative and drive. People recognized that it was important to have a place in town to share food.

Jesus also recognized the importance of sharing food. There are a great many stories in the Gospels about his sharing food with others. One of the few incidents that occurs in all four Gospels is the story about Jesus dividing the loaves and fishes until there was enough to feed four or five thousand people, a story with Eucharistic overtones (Matt. 14:13–21; 15:32–39; Mark 6:30–44; Luke 9:10–17; John 6:1–13). We often don't realize how many occasions there are in our congregations when people come together enticed by refreshments being offered. There is power in sharing food—among friends and relatives, but also with strangers. The latter practice is called "hospitality" in the Christian tradition, but it has little to do with silver services or the etiquette of a good hostess. Indeed, Tom Ogletree and Christine Pohl,[1] among others, have emphasized that hospitality, sharing what we have with strangers, is a central Christian practice. Maybe it is even *the* central Christian practice (see, for example, 1 Peter 4:8–9). In this chapter I want to consider how food and sharing go together.

First, food and sharing go together in the routine, everyday way we share food with friends and relatives, neighbors, and church members. Second, food and sharing get expressed in hospitality to those beyond our kinship or friendship group. Hospitality is offered to strangers for reasons that have almost nothing to do with that person or group and everything to do with the fact that sharing—even with strangers—is a natural response to the gratitude and joy we feel to God. It mirrors God's own hospitality and makes family out of strangers.

Thus I consider in this chapter the two interlocked practices of *sharing* (which is restricted here to sharing with people we know) and *hospitality* (which extends sharing to include people who are strangers or in some cases even enemies). I would like to include the understanding of community here as well, but that would expand the chapter beyond meaningful bounds. Instead, I will consider community in chapter 4, where the practice of celebrating is lifted up, and deal here with the practice of sharing with friends, relatives, and acquaintances.

Sharing

Sharing food is perhaps the primary socializing and civilizing activity of human beings. Eating is far more than merely taking on fuel, which it is for a frog snagging a fly or a cow munching grass. In its special issue on "Overcoming Obesity,"[2] *Time* magazine reported, "To a human, the ritual of eating . . . is one of the most primal of shared activities. We eat together when we celebrate. . . . We solve our problems over the family dinner table, conduct our business over the executive lunch table, entertain guests over cake and cookies at the coffee table."[3] "Interaction over food is the single most important feature of socializing," says Sidney Mintz, professor of anthropology at Johns Hopkins University. "The food becomes the carriage that conveys feelings back and forth."[4]

Beyond this, however, sharing food is a central custom among all ethnic groups. It is also a central component of regional identity. Foods define who we are as a particular people. We still cook cheese grits in our house and thereby retain our Southern roots. Patti introduced the family to Mexican cuisine from her California years, and this has become a favorite with us as well. Italian cuisine, Jewish, Norwegian, Cantonese—each reminds us of particular events and peoples. The stronger the ethnic identity, the more this is the case. The Italians, for example, say that it is around the table that friends understand best the warmth of being together.[5]

Many commentators, myself included, are upset because eating together (sharing food) seems to be in decline in the United States and also elsewhere around the world, particularly in affluent nations. What is the source of our concern? Why is sharing that important? Why the upset about eating together being in decline?

The Centrality of Sharing Food

Do you remember when you were encouraged (probably by your mother) to share your toys or your candy? Why was that? I believe that even at that early age and stage you and I were being socialized to interact with others in ways that are central to our well-being. Indeed, my much stronger conviction is that an absolutely central, nonvoluntary, foundational part of our human nature is that we are related to others.[6] Indeed, if we attend to our physical eco-nature, we see, as David Abram pointed out, that we are at the core of our being interdependent with all kinds of others—human, plant, mineral, animal, and cosmic.[7] Aristotle, Thomas Aquinas, Margaret Mead, G. H. Mead, and all sorts of classical thinkers have said that. Never, however, has that been so evident as it is in our world, where Al-Quaida terrorists half a world away sneeze and the country goes on orange alert, or the quality of the soybean harvest in Brazil is watched closely by farmers in Nebraska.

The ways in which we share our very identity and bodily presence with others is much more primal than global interdependence may suggest. Indeed, we could not even be human at all without such sharing with others. Added to that, consider the fact that eating is itself a daily routine, something we anticipate and usually enjoy. Moreover, eating is a prime requisite of life. These two primal activities—food and sharing—are linked. Family connections, business negotiations, celebrations, and meeting newcomers all are enhanced when these relationships are undertaken with a good meal. Thus, their very primacy leads to their association.

We who are alarmed at the decline of eating together by families see the ability to share food at home as a foundation of interpersonal, social, and public life.[8] Eating together is one antidote to individual-ism; sharing is a school of sociability. Thus, not to share at home con-stitutes a loss of our mutuality. Over time this leads to an inability to share and contributes to an inability to be mutually accountable. To the extent that this is true, there is also a weakening of our voluntary association with others, such as community groups, the church, or political parties.[9] There is a spiraling down of our capacity to relate to others. Interpersonal sharing leads to third-sector association and is also the foundation of *hospitality* to strangers.

Alternately, eating together can spiral up and enable people to share in ever-widening circles of openness. We become more capable of mutual accountability in this way.[10] We are formed in being open to diverse opinions and people when we share food. In the Christian community, we are under mandate to love neighbors as ourselves in an ever-expanding inclusiveness.[11] Given the formative power of sharing, not to eat together carries a loss in the ability to share on a personal level, participate in voluntary associations, and be engaged in civic life. Eating together—at home, at church, at a political rally—builds our ability to associate with others.

Christian Sharing

Up to this point, I have said little that is explicitly Christian about sharing. Indeed, Christians believe that sharing is a central practice, but it seems clear that sharing is close to the core of being truly human, whatever one's beliefs. A strong case can be made on purely secular grounds that sharing is a practice that is integral to human nature and well-being. For reasons both social and biological, sharing is vital to human health. This does not depend on particular beliefs.[12] At this juncture, however, I consider some of the reasons why Christians in particular consider sharing to be a gracious mandate and a joy.

1. *Sharing is natural.* It is natural to share because God created human beings to be in relationship with God, with other men and women,

and with the rest of the created order. Douglas John Hall asserts that one cannot ask about the character of human beings in isolation. Indeed, "[t]his being has its being—no, receives its being—as it stands in relationship with God and with its own kind and with 'otherkind' (i.e., non- or extra-human creatures)."[13] Consider also the statement of Daniel Migliore that "in the act of creation, God already manifests the self-communicating, other-affirming, community-forming love that defines God's eternal triune reality and that is decisively disclosed in the ministry and sacrificial death of Jesus Christ" (and through the work of the Holy Spirit).[14]

2. *Sharing produces joy.* Christians consider sharing to be a joy because relating to others enters into our very constitution. Just as there are distinct persons in the Trinity, no one of whom can be understood apart from the other, so also we human beings are defined by our relating to and sharing with others. Monika Hellwig makes evident the meaning of this claim about humankind being created in the image of the triune, inter-communicating God. Men and women have a need, a drive, a hunger to share that—if unfulfilled—renders them incomplete. In short, we need to share. It is our joy to share.[15]

Hellwig suggests that there is no human growth into wholeness without "learning to move out of the limelight, to acknowledge others as persons, to find satisfaction in giving and serving and spending oneself for others."[16] In short, we cannot be whole beings without sharing. This may be difficult for those whose lives fall into contemporary patterns. With the ease and convenience of meeting physical needs, today's affluent people have "little experience of the inevitability of sharing, because more is bought and more always seems to be there to be bought."[17] But genuine wholeness requires sharing with other people, sharing oneself, sharing possessions, sharing food.

3. *Wholeness entails sharing.* In short, wholeness or salvation involves sharing. This may sound simple, but there are clear prerequisites that must precede (or conditions that must underlie) genuine sharing. Children, for example, may need to receive and to learn to trust

before they can share. The church has a significant role to play in this aspect of Christian formation. There are other prerequisites, I suspect, and they deserve investigation.

Genuine sharing is akin to the giving of gifts or serving others; it is not just the performance of acts. Instead, attitude counts. One's attitude in sharing is part of the act of sharing itself. We must be able to share, to let go, to be dependent—precisely those things that a moneyed people find that they have been insulating themselves against. We have learned how not to share, and we are losing the ability to share.

4. *Fortunately, we can relearn sharing.* That will necessitate starting where we are, with diminished capacity. However, we can begin every day by learning to share food, a very simple but profound experience. We begin by practicing sharing, and we maintain that skill by practicing. It takes sharing in order to divide up the tasks of preparing meals, to get everyone together, to coordinate the gathering of the food, to say grace, to eat at the same time, and to share the experiences of the day along with the food. Sharing is, quite simply, a way of checking in, of sharing oneself along with the food. It is striking to me that this checking in is an important thing to do virtually every day; if I fail to check in every day with my wife or teenager, I begin to lose involvement in their lives. Furthermore, it is usually a way of planning the future, of learning what the others will be doing as well as have been doing. It also contributes to reflection; sharing with and conversing with others helps refine my thinking and make it objective to me. As sharing builds up, I am prepared to face myself by sharing with others and becoming able to receive from them—even criticism. I am willing to trust that that criticism is constructive. Having learned that, I may be willing to risk sharing constructive criticism *and even affirmation.* Others may be willing to affirm me as well.

As you perceive, this process is gradual. It may begin by simply being an action with the hope that a change in attitude will accompany the act. But, as sharing proceeds, the action may in fact lead to a changing attitude. We may find that we enjoy sharing, indeed, that we find fulfillment there. This is a building process, but one that I am persuaded will lead to greater enjoyment.

Two questions arise: (1) Is it necessary to share *food*? Are there not other things one could share that would lead to the development of this skill? I believe the answer to this is yes, but. . . . Yes, but it is hard to imagine sharing without food being involved, without eating together. Can you relate to others without eating with them? Yes, you could, but why would you want to? Sharing food is the simplest way, the most natural way to begin the act of building up a relationship where deeper sharing becomes possible. It is an activity that we engage in three or more times a day. It may be the practice of sharing that is most available and most effective (and most enjoyable!).

(2) The last issue here is, Why family and friends? Why limit the sharing of food to family and friends as I have been doing to this point in the chapter? My reason for beginning with sharing and limiting the use of that term to our interaction with family and friends is that I think sharing with family and friends is where we learn the art of sharing. The home and the associated friendships are schools of virtue where we learn the practices necessary for abundant life. Sharing is such a practice. I now turn to a consideration of sharing with others beyond our family and friends—or hospitality.

Hospitality

It may seem at least unusual to reserve the term *hospitality* for strangers, to sharing with those whom we don't know—even those who are marginal. Sharing with enemies may be beyond our imagination. For Christians, however, the tradition of hospitality goes far beyond the contemporary restriction of the word primarily to refer to the way we receive family and friends. As Henri Nouwen put it, hospitality conjures up the image of "tea parties, bland conversation, and a general atmosphere of coziness. . . . [But] if there is any concept worth restoring to its original depth and evocative potential, it is the concept of hospitality."[18] In many ways, thanks to such authors as Thomas Ogletree, Christine Pohl, and, of course, Nouwen himself, the concept is being restored to its original bite and edginess. For the Hebrews, failure to welcome the stranger and sojourner could lead to disastrous, life-threatening consequences. Seeing themselves as strangers and sojourners, moreover, made this mandate to care for the vulnerable and those at risk in their midst a foundational part of their identity as the people of God. As a slave people, a people at risk, they understood that hospitality was a matter of life and death, not coziness or light banter. In their harsh climate, not to welcome the nomad was to treat the other completely contrary to how God had treated them (see Lev. 19:34). Their response of gratitude to God took the form of treating others with hospitality, just as God had treated them.

It is clear that Jesus practiced precisely this kind of hospitality, even to his death. No one was excluded from his table fellowship. Jesus himself often depended on the hospitality of others, and even—it might be claimed—saw the receiving of hospitality as a gift that matches the giving of hospitality. He acted both as host and guest. Surely his practice of eating with every kind of person—his closest friends, the disciples, Samaritan women, tax collectors, and the disreputable—stands as a witness to the centrality of hospitality to the gospel.

The early church also put a high value on the practice of offering hospitality to strangers. They were people of the Way. As Christine Pohl puts it, "Early Christian writers claimed that transcending social and ethnic differences by sharing meals, homes, and worship with persons of different backgrounds was a proof of the truth of the Christian faith."[19] Often this hospitality was extended to other Christians, as we know from the epistles of Paul. Early Christians understood that hospitality included physical, social, and spiritual dimensions of human experience. "In almost every case," Pohl writes, "hospitality involved shared meals; historically, table fellowship was an important way of recognizing the equal value and dignity of persons."[20]

Martin Luther, John Calvin, John Wesley, and many other Christian thinkers have seen hospitality as a ministry to Christ himself.[21] So when persecuted believers were received hospitably, Luther claimed that "God himself is in our home, is being fed at our table." Calvin taught that no act was "more pleasing or acceptable to God" than receiving religious refugees into believers' homes. This was a "sacred" form of hospitality for Calvin; he encouraged believers to see in strangers the image of God and our common flesh. Similarly, John Wesley resisted all attempts to weaken or explain away Matthew 25:31–46, the mandate to feed the hungry, clothe the naked, and visit those in prison as though those people were Christ himself.[22]

Experiencing Hospitality

In many respects, hospitality is akin to sharing with family and friends. But we can identify its central differentiating features.

1. *Hospitality is welcoming.* We know very well the difference between being welcomed warmly and not being welcomed or being welcomed only lukewarmly. We know the value of hospitality to family and friends; the distinctive practice of Christian hospitality was to extend the circle of those welcomed to include the poor and marginalized. The close relations fostered by table fellowship and conversation were expanded to strangers. Just as family and friends flourish in the context of a warm welcome and a hospitable meal, so also do those at church, the homeless, the disabled, the displaced, and even strangers and enemies.

2. *Hospitality involves the recognition of the dignity and value of others.* One of Christine Pohl's central points in her remarkable book is that hospitality recognizes the others. This recognition makes all the difference between feeling like someone and the widespread sense among the poor and marginalized that they are "nobody." Hospitality recognizes the other and conveys dignity.

When my sons and I worked at the Dorothy Day House in Minnesota, it was important for us not just to bring or prepare the food.

We needed to involve the "guests" in the preparation and also to eat with and visit with the guests as we ate. To have remained withdrawn would be to practice a hospitality of the distanced—which is almost an oxymoron. This was no doubt the most difficult part of the experience because we didn't know what to expect. Most important, we didn't know whether the guests would accept us. We were in the position of being vulnerable, just as they were. Actually we are all interdependent all the time (in far less vulnerable and material ways than the homeless, to be sure), and it is helpful for us to experience it.

Churches may need to find ways to interact with those they "serve" or to whom they make donations. If they do not, they may thereby be depriving themselves of what they could learn from others who are different. They may be short-circuiting their own formation by ignoring the whole persons whom they are to love as themselves.

Perhaps it is this dignity and recognition that enable people to live a reputable, respectful life. Partly attitude, partly action, recognition means meeting the other as a person whose dynamics are as complicated and whose life is as complex as one's own. This suggests a humility and compassion that is born out of an alertness to the ways in which we have been graced and how little our position depends on our own doing. This may also foster a forgiveness of enemies.

3. *Hospitality usually involves eating* (you saw that coming). In part, this is an expression of our basic equality and the fact that we all have basic needs. We share a common humanity, so that the differences of rich and poor, black and white, young and old, brown and yellow, male and female are not wiped out but placed in a wider context of need and humanity and joy of relating.

It is also true that many people in our world are hungry. To be sure, we are confronted with the hungry and homeless in our cities and towns, but it is helpful for us to see in them the wider face of world hunger. Eating with and feeding people is urgent for those without adequate food. As my friend Ed Loring, who works at the

Open Door in Atlanta, likes to say, "Justice is important, but supper is essential."[23] The fact of world hunger at home and abroad is on the agenda of every Christian church, as it should be. Besides the command to "Feed the hungry," the need to eat reminds us of the communal nature of the lives we share with all other species, including our own. Many claim that insuring that all people are adequately fed, clothed, and sheltered *should* be on the top of the agenda of every nation as well as every church. Practicing hospitality is a matter of justice as well as of love.

4. *Hospitality is essential to human well-being.* We all need hospitality; we need to receive it and we need to give it. The claim that only by sharing can we experience wholeness applies to hospitality as well. Jesus asked his disciples, "For if you love those who love you, what reward do you have? Do not even the tax collectors do the same? And if you greet only your brothers and sisters, what more are you doing than others? Do not even the Gentiles do the same?" (Matt. 5:46–47). Luke adds, "But love your enemies, do good, and lend, expecting nothing in return. Your reward will be great, and you will be children of the Most High; for he is kind to the ungrateful and the wicked" (Luke 6:35). The church has drawn the quite logical conclusion that we are to share with all people.

Being in relationship with God and with others is integral to human wholeness. Being able to be hospitable with others is our grateful response to the hospitality of God. "Hospitality becomes for the Christian community a way of being the sacrament of God's love in the world."[24]

There is also in hospitality a "complex dance between recognizing our own need, ministering to those in need, and recognizing their ministry to us."[25] Hospitality is done not simply out of duty. We are empowered by offering hospitality to others; we realize that we are enriched by those others as well. We recognize our own need, and that helps us realize that respect is not abrogated by homelessness or need. We see that we have needs that are disguised by our material abundance. The perspective that hospitality offers on material possessions and simplicity of lifestyle is also a freedom from overidentifying our worth with our status of any kind. Eating together is a concrete symbol of this. It expresses the basic worth of each person and reveals to us that we exist in relationship with others and God. We may have become so individualistic in our thinking that we fail to appreciate activities that build community. We may not understand how important community is for giving us life. Perhaps hospitality is such a practice. We can appreciate its value for our well-being by noting that it creates community and that hospitality is best sustained by communities. Those communities allow *us* to blossom and grow and witness to the world. They might even give us a glimpse of what the kingdom might look like.

Hospitality is making room for others. As we welcome others into our rooms, we find that community begins to develop. We have more, we receive more, we share more, and rather than being diminished we build up community. Being in relation with others is where we live more deeply than what we own or who we are. Being in life together with God and the world is our home. Hospitality is finally a life-giving practice; it helps create communities where both host and guest are recognized and affirmed. In breaking bread together, we begin to experience God's energy.

Learning to Be Hospitable

Hospitality to strangers is certainly not an abstract theological topic. Instead, it bridges our theology with our everyday world, where sharing with family and friends comes more easily than sharing with strangers. Sharing and hospitality are, of course, siblings. The actual practice of hospitality, rather than mere discussions about hospitality, gives life and vitality to faith. Abstract discussions of hospitality may serve to disguise the performative nature of the concept. It might even be said that they violate the spirit of the word, and certainly they violate the practice. Talking about hospitality without practicing it may mean that we literally don't know what we are talking about! Confronting our own prejudices and fears about being hospitable raises significant faith questions for us. Can we genuinely share our eating with strangers? Are we willing to share, trusting that there will be enough for all? Can we trust that others will be hospitable to us?

I have now left the realm of *talking* about hospitality and take up the task of learning to *be* hospitable. As every tennis player or pianist knows, we become proficient at a particular skill by practicing it regularly and by learning from those who are already masters. Hospitality is such a skill and a practice, but it is different from those others in that it is an action suffused with attitude. It is a practice that has roots in so many other areas of life, in our character and our commitments, that its growth also causes these other areas to grow and flourish. We learn to be hospitable to others, to strangers and to our friends and relatives—at a certain point, maybe even to ourselves.

Hospitality is a way of being in the world, an orientation to others and to life itself. It is a means of grace, a way both of receiving God's grace and being in tune with the gracious life of the world. It is a way of passing on God's grace and being graced in return. It is a welcoming and sustaining way of life.

We can begin to learn such grace and such welcoming, slowly. First, we might *think* about sharing and hospitality. The following activities are designed to help us think about and then get a feel for hospitality.

1. Sharing and hospitality are old concepts with an important presence in every culture in some form. When company comes, whether it is strangers, family or friends, why do people welcome each other with food and drink? How are hospitality traditions alike and how are they different? What are their origins? Personally, what makes you feel welcome and why? What role does food play in the experience? Do people ever use food or beverages to communicate a word that is far more intimate than the act of sharing?

2. One classic New Testament story about hospitality is that of the Good Samaritan (Luke 10:29–37). Enact the story of the Good Samaritan. Discuss the roles of the Samaritan and the victim. How does each feel? What was the Samaritan's motivation? What did you learn from this story when you thought beneath the surface?

3. Think about a time in life when you received hospitality. Did receiving such hospitality make any difference in your life? How did it feel? Did it make a difference in your community's life?

    Can you recall a time when you gave hospitality to others— on a mission trip or when your youth group worked at the rescue mission or shelter in your town? What sort of feelings did you have before that experience? During the experience? How do you look back on it?

    Do you feel as though God was involved in either the experience of receiving hospitality or giving it? Were you aware that you were sharing hospitality rather than just receiving or giving hospitality?

4. In the book *Teaching Kids to Care and Share: 300+ Mission and Service Ideas for Children*, Jolene Roehikepartain begins with some principles that are equally useful for adults in learning sharing and hospitality.[26] Her keys are:

    - Make projects concrete. Use your senses. Be tactical.
    - Work with existing networks. No need to siphon off energy.
    - Empower children (and adults). With real, difference-making projects.
    - Debrief children (adults) about experiences afterward.
    - Line up your resources.
    - Dovetail the project with your church's mission.
    - Have fun (this is even more important for adults).[27]

The following activities are for persons of all ages. Adults can make cookies for shut-ins; children can explore what happens to leftover food from the school cafeteria or local restaurants.

5. The scriptures provide thoughtful experiences that touch on hospitality:

   - Exodus 2:16–22. Moses hides, and people seek him out to invite him to eat. Children sometimes are shy and hide at mealtime. It is important to eat and share together. Work with children to prepare simple drinks to share at a church function or with others at a social occasion.
   - Mark 6:30–44. Jesus feeds the five thousand. Ask how children think those loaves and fishes were enough to feed five thousand. Then pass around a bagel or doughnut and ask everyone to break off just a bit so that everyone will have some. Many communities have occasions when they feed the homeless. Encourage children and adults to participate in these activities. Bake bread together and share the baking with people at church or others who are needy in the community.
   - Genesis 27:1–10. Focus on the significance of cooking and food in the story. As a group, make a pizza for lunch, eat together, and then talk about the significance of both the preparation and the eating.

6. Adult conversation and activity might center on both contemplation and action:

Questions for Thought

1. Do you think that Monika Hellwig is right when she claims that human beings have a need to share with others? Why or why not?

2. Do you think that human beings, especially adults, have a need to receive from others?
3. Do you think that, as a people, we are losing the ability to share?
4. If you think sharing is essential to our humanity and that we are losing that ability, what does that portend?
5. How do giving and receiving relate to our faith in God?

Action Projects

1. Explore the fate of food left over from restaurants or grocery stores or school cafeterias. Who in the community would benefit from receiving this food?
2. What else might a group do to feed the hungry in the community?
3. Plan or support a mission trip. Be a part of the team.
4. Support the work of organizations that are hospitable, such as local chapters of Bread for the World, www. bread.org.
5. Find out how the Foods Resource Bank works to link urban and rural Christians with each other and with international food projects, www.foodresourcebank.com.
6. Explore the ministry of Heifer Project International, www .heifer.org.
7. Get connected with a local campaign to distribute food to shelters, rescue missions, and food pantries.

FOUR

Feasting in Community

*When Jesus calls us to abundant life, he calls us to experience life
as a feast, a feast of meanings, a feast of opportunities, and a feast of
possibilities. To be invited to such a feast is to make Eucharist, to offer
thanks for divine and diverse epiphanies of love that nurture toward
well-being. Would that more of us could welcome his invitation.*[1]

IT ONLY HAPPENS ONCE in a lifetime.

My birthday is July 23—a rather nondescript day. This particular
birthday, the kids were coming home for my sixtieth, and we decided
to play golf that afternoon. That was very nice, and I was looking
forward to it.

When we got home, I was pretty oblivious. As I was going up
the stairs in my sweat-soaked T-shirt, I heard a loud scream, "Happy
Birthday!" and saw a huge crowd. There were Joe Maw and Al Fer-
rer from South San Francisco; Al and Martha Beattie from Palmdale,
California; Phil and Ann Jung from Mobile, Alabama; Susan, Bill,
Pauline, and Dave from Loyola in Chicago; friends from the University of Dubuque and Wartburg seminaries; neighbors and friends
from Dubuque; the kids' friends; and others. My mom was already at
our house visiting, so she was in the crowd as well.

Yes, I was surprised. But that was just the beginning. Patti had the
event catered, and the food was terrific—hors d'oeuvres of bacon-
wrapped chestnuts, little sandwiches, good champagne, and a really
fine meal. Too much.

A feast, a celebration—not something one deserves. It only happens once in a lifetime. It was great, a blessing beyond anything I could imagine.

There's another story that needs to supplement this one. It is rather humble, but it is important to review. Dick Poppen, a farmer friend from Bancroft, South Dakota, tells it.

Rounding the corner of our farmhouse recently, we were surprised to discover a variety of creatures—three ducks, a few chickens, and two cats—enjoying the contents of the dog's dish. The dog, either adequately sated or unusually polite, observed from a distance. We were reminded of the vision of the peaceful kingdom:

But with righteousness he shall judge the poor,
and decide with equity for the meek
of the earth. . . .
the wolf shall live with the lamb,
the leopard shall lie down with the kid,
the calf and the lion and the fatling together,
and a little child shall lead them.
The cow and the bear shall graze,
their young shall lie down together.
(Isa. 11:4a, 6-7a)

Participation at the banquet can be a time of fighting, hoarding, discrimination, and deprivation. Or—guided by the vision of the peaceful kingdom of God, directed by appropriate regulation, and driven by the decree to enjoy and celebrate the variety of contributors—participation can be a celebration of life. It can be a demonstration of God's love for the world and all who dwell in it.

Pondering why the members of our farm's menagerie were all so willing to share a dish that day, we considered the possibility that each animal was aware that it did not own it. Each had come as a guest. No one owns the banquet.[2]

Feasting has fallen into disrepute. In a religion suffused with the reality of resurrection, liberation, deliverance, grace, and celebration, one might expect feasting to be a central practice. And it used to be. For us, however, feasting tends to connote more of what we already have too much of—food piled on top of more food. Our problem is too much rather than too little. I am persuaded that the origins of this disrepair are profound and potent.

Feasting is a communal practice of celebration. In the church, and in the culture, feasting has become a rare occurrence because we do not know much about celebrating (except overcelebrating or self-indulging—again, too much alcohol or food or drugs) because we are not comfortable in community. We simply do not delight very well. Lest this appear irredeemable, let me hasten to suggest that food offers us the possibility of relearning how to feast. That will take some doing, of course.

There is an essential truth underlying affluent people's sense that simply eating and drinking in excess does not constitute a feast. Rather, the act of feasting arises from the celebration of a community. Thus the broader issue concerns the strength of community and our ability to take delight, to celebrate together, to make community together.

In the post–9/11 climate of national security and war, we have become fearful as a people. Fear has a tendency to destroy social bonds and threaten relations of trust. In a culture where a sense of community was already attenuated, fear can heighten our individualism and render celebration even more problematic. Our feasting may be limited to family or institutional settings.

Sources of Loss

In this chapter I explore briefly what has happened to our ability to feast. Then I turn to the spiritual practice of celebration—the ability to enjoy, to delight, to approach life with zest and confidence. The last section focuses on relearning the practice of feasting.

How did we get to this place, especially in a culture that seems to claim that there is a way (be it pill or commodity or diversion) to avoid all pain and find only pleasure and happiness? We have lost much of the ability to delight because (1) we cannot face the reality of negation and loss, and also because, (2) while we know we cannot engender happiness by dint of any or everything that we can do, we find it hard to imagine that happiness might happen without our producing it. This takes various forms, but they coalesce in the belief that we can *do* something (or *take* something) to produce joy. We don't know any alternative route for dealing with frustration, disappointment, tragedy, or any other lack of happiness. (3) A third reason has to do with our complicity, however involuntary, in the suffering of others. It is difficult to enjoy pleasures that come at the expense of others.

Focusing on the reasons why we have difficulty delighting is especially pertinent in a chapter on celebrating and feasting. Here's what I think: Celebrating takes a certain amount of spontaneity; spontaneity makes the difference between an "occasion" and a feast. If we cannot trust the people we are with, we cannot be spontaneous. The breakdown of community lessens the degree of trust we feel. When social trust and communal feeling break down, our ability to celebrate and delight is lessened. Wholehearted feasting is rare.

Competitiveness and protectiveness are likewise antithetical to feasting. When we feel that we are in competition with others for scarce resources—be they winning seasons, status, jobs, or whatever, our capacity to delight with them is diminished. Likewise, when we are insecure by reason of economics, terrorism, or diffuse vulnerability, we cannot feast. We United States citizens have become aware from experience that we really cannot produce security or happiness. We cannot shut out all threats any more than we can control all factors or produce joy. The unmasking of this functional illusion has thrown us into a search for feasible alternatives.

Just a word about the effect of complicity on our celebrating: When we sense that our own eating high on the hog comes at the expense of others' eating at all, then we cannot feast. This may be a good thing, especially if we recognize that we are called to reverse the inequity of benefiting from others' pain. Too often, we simply walk by on the other side and try to avoid conscious reflection on injustice. However much it may dampen the current impulse to feast, recognition of complicity may eventually engender a more genuine feast. This makes us aware that feasting is a matter of attitude as much as it is a matter of the quality and quantity of food.

Thus far we have been describing the *cultural* sources of the loss of capacity for feasting. These no doubt infiltrate Christian attitudes and practices.[3] It is instructive to look specifically at what has happened to Christian celebrations.

The central "feast" of the Christian faith is the Eucharist, the Lord's Supper, but the countercultural nature of that Lord's Supper may be disappearing. June Goudey charges that

> while the remembrance of Jesus' death, not the healing power of his life, became the primary premise of the eucharist, our attention turned in upon the elements and away from the table-fellowship of those gathered. As a result, a powerful, celebratory, and communal meal began a steady evolution into an individualistic and penitential rite.[4]

We may in fact altogether forget that the Eucharist is a celebration.

> The Lord's Supper in most of our churches ... is a solemn affair marked by sad, mournful, even morbid thoughts associated with death. It is more like a fast than a feast. It bears little

resemblance to the banquet which the father prepared for his lost son. It seems we can no longer partake of food with glad and generous hearts. . . .[5]

This feast has become so attenuated that we sometimes overlook the fact that it involves drinking and eating at all. What kind of poor feast is it that consists of a thin wafer or bit of Wonder Bread and a thimble of wine or grape juice? Arthur Cochrane suggests that the "simplest and most necessary reform of the Lord's Supper in our congregations is that it must become a meal for the nourishment of the physical body."[6] Why? Because this meal is "a sign of the grace of creation and preservation." Thus, there "should be bread and wine in abundance, so that everyone may have as much as he or she needs."[7]

The Eucharist also has become separated from the agape feast, which was celebrated as a full meal in the very early church.[8] Furthermore, the Eucharist has become far more exclusive than inclusive, and yet part of the heart of Eucharist gains its meaning from the inclusive table fellowship of Jesus.[9] Finally, the Eucharist once had a missional element, witnessing to Christ's saving power to the larger, public world, which it now has largely lost.

I must conclude that, as a model of feasting, the Eucharist as it is currently practiced is not really helpful. Frankly, it didn't occur to me to be a contender for the model for the practice of feasting. It is far too staid, too ritualized, too removed from joyous celebration. I shall return to the Lord's Supper in chapter 8. However, there are better sources for rehabilitating the practice of celebrative, communal feasting than the Eucharist as presently practiced. Perhaps by developing those sources we can begin to flesh out the Eucharist.

Christian Feasting

There are few contemporary examples to draw upon in describing feasting. First, I look to biblical and theological foundations for a more vivid description of what enters into this practice.

In a sermon preached in 1728, Jonathan Edwards spoke of "The Spiritual Blessings of the Gospel Represented by a Feast."[10] He used the prophecy of the great banquet in Isaiah 25:6 ("On this mountain the LORD of hosts will make for all peoples a feast of rich food") and Jesus' parables in Luke 14:16 ("Someone gave a great dinner and invited many") and Luke 15:23 (the feast the forgiving father gave to the prodigal son). Edwards's point is that the gospel can be seen as a feast, and the feast as a sign of God's blessing. In a sermon contemporary to that one, Edwards spoke of "the pleasantness of religion."[11] There he asserted that "God has given us of his redundant bounty many things for the delight of our senses. . . . Religion allows us to take the full comfort of our meat and drink. . . ." Indeed, Edwards claimed that the religious person "enjoys spiritual pleasures that are much better and sweeter than any others. . . ; there is much the most delight in a religious life. . . ."[12]

Of interest to me is Edwards's clear association of sensual, physical pleasures with spiritual blessings as "gospel pleasures." He valorizes and holds feasts in esteem as a source of delight. In short, and always within reason, Edwards affirms the practice of feasting.

In this Edwards is entirely in the tradition of Israelite feasting in the Old Testament. Feasting had a prominent role in hospitality and the bonding of families then and also in promoting a sense of community. Feasting "played an important part in the life of Israel" according to Sara Covin Juengst. "It became a primary way to express covenant renewal, as the people sat at table with God to reaffirm the bonds of obligation and kinship."[13] The feasts of Passover and Unleavened Bread, of Weeks (for Christians, Pentecost), and the Feast of Booths were all celebrations of Yahweh's providence and expressed joy and thanksgiving to God. They gave strength and cohesion to the people of Israel.[14] These feasts were continued in the New Testament and early church practice in general. The Passover, Lord's Supper, and Pentecost stand out, as do Jesus' many parables about banquets (Matt. 22:1–10, Luke 14:15–24) and the great feast of restoration (Rev. 3:20; 19:7–9; 22:17). Finally, it appears that Jesus himself practiced feasting.

Elements of Feasting

From all these materials about celebration and feasting we begin to discover some common features. The present section of the chapter will attempt a formulation of the central features of feasting.

1. Feasting is *joy-full*. Richard Foster puts a high premium on the value of celebration in the Christian life: "Celebration is at the heart of the way of Christ."[15] Celebration brings joy into our lives, and joy—especially shared joy such as happens at feasts—gives us strength. Foster places the discipline of celebration at the end of his book *Celebration of Discipline* because "joy is the end result of the Spiritual Disciplines' functioning in our lives. God brings about the transformation of our lives through the Disciplines, and we will not know genuine joy until there is a transforming work within us."[16] We cannot force ourselves to feel genuine joy through feasting or any other means. However, we can open ourselves to God's transforming work. How to do that will be the focus of the closing section of this chapter.

2. Feasting is *doxological*. Feasting cannot be about *us*; it is about the celebrative worship of God. It is an expression of joy that is at the very core of our discipleship. It gathers up a world of meanings that we then live out of and live out every day. It is festival. If feasting is about us, then it will scarcely get off the ground. Discipleship, or worship, springs from joy and feeds joy. "The joy Jesus offers his disciples is his own joy, which flows from his intimate communion with the one who sent him."[17]

Foster suggests that celebration arises from *obedience* to God. Though we seldom associate "celebration" and "obedience" in our public discourse, Cathy Campbell makes a similar assertion: "This delight-full sense of joy in the path of life and in the decrees, laws, or road-map for our God-walk is not always associated with the life of faith . . . [or with] a festive feast." But if the law of the Lord (Ps. 19:7–10) is understood as part of our connection to God, as an invitation, "it is all about the joy of the banquet."[18]

This joy in the Christian life goes beyond the transitory happiness of good fortune or achievement; and it is not deflated by misfortune or even negation. Instead, it can be described as a profound sense of wholeness, of life abundant, salvation. It comes from the worship of God and a life given in obedience to God. We feast, then, out of a sense of completeness, of life lived from the center. This is authentic celebration of the good things of life given by God. It recognizes the ongoing creativity that grows in us as we walk with God. That is joy indeed.

3. Feasting grows out of *a sense of God's abundance and generosity.* Because feasting is in the first place a blessing of God, who is the source of food and all life and sustenance, it is an acknowledgment of "God's bounty and generosity."[19] The banquet of the kingdom is all about abundance and fecundity. It is an exuberant recognition of God's mammoth surplus of love and goodness. Poor people may have a richer sense of feasting out of an appreciation of God's abundance.

One of the reasons we may have trouble feasting is because our human economy is premised on scarcity. We hoard for fear of not having enough. Walter Brueggemann has demonstrated in clear contrast that the God of Scripture is a God of abundance. "Creation is primarily an exuberant, lyrical, doxological expression of gratitude and amazement for the goodness and generosity of God. . . . There is more than enough. There is as much as the limitless, self-giving God can imagine."[20] Does a sense of scarcity or of abundance dominate our emotional as well as economic imagination? Maybe we Christians could learn to dance and sing more.

This abundance and generosity is particularly visible in the fact that all are invited to Jesus' banquet. The feast is set for all, but the blind, the poor, and the lame are those who accept the invitation first (Luke 14:12; cf. Deut. 10:17–19). The feast that Jesus images is the feast of a gift economy where absolutely all are included. The reality of famine, malnutrition, poverty, disease, and starvation has no part in that vision. Rather, we are to work to minimize scarcity in the midst of abundance. We pray, "Your kingdom come, your will be done, on earth as in heaven."

4. Feasting is *a communal celebration* that transforms us. Pat McCormick suggests that most Americans do not know what they

are doing when they eat, because our unconscious way of eating has cut us off from the "religious" or relational meaning of food.[21] How then could we understand feasting, since its very nature is communal celebration?

Christianity grew out of a Jewish tradition rich with communal festivals and feasts. It is little wonder that eating and drinking together marked the early apostolic community (see Acts 2:42–46). Veronica E. Grimm has done us the great service of showing how a tradition rich in feasting came to emphasize fasting instead. "The early texts . . . show a natural, matter-of-fact acceptance of food and eating and emphasize the social importance of food in conviviality, in enhancing the feeling of brotherhood and as a gesture conveying mutual acceptance into the Christian group."[22] Alexander Schmemann sees the Christian practice of feasting as a result of its being "born and preached first in cultures in which feasts and celebrations were an organic and essential part of the whole world-view and way of life. . . . And, whether we like it or not, Christianity *accepted* and made its own this fundamentally human phenomenon of feast, as it accepted and made its own the whole [hu]man and all [their] needs."[23] At its heart, feasting is a communal celebration expressing shared joy.

When we probe the boundaries of community, there is an expansive dynamic fueled by Jesus' commission to reach out into all the world. To be sure, the feasting community begins with the body of Christ (the church family), which already stretches the bounds of biological family, but it extends—at least potentially—to all of God's children and to the creation itself. Feasting is both an outgrowth of reconciliation and unity within the community and also a spur toward greater reconciliation and unity.

Feasting reminds us of community and, beyond the immediate community, the common hunger and delight of eating that we share with all people. The generosity and abundance associated with feasting also leads to transformation. The sheer magnitude of grace reflected in Christian feasting makes us yearn to share that feast, both

spiritually and physically, with others. We get a glimpse of the kingdom and want to share.

Gordon Lathrop reminds us that Christians share a "hungry feast"
that recognizes that Christ stands in solidarity with the hungry of the
world.[24] Our feasting is juxtaposed with fasting and intensified by
fasting. We are transformed by our peculiar feasts to see the "web of
interdependent relationship" and begin to know that "if one member suffers, all suffer together with it; if one member is honored, all
rejoice together with it."[25]

My claim is that authentic feasting gives us a view of the world
in which solidarity with others is more fundamental than how I am
doing financially or professionally. It can—occasionally and fleetingly—help us see that solidarity where our *common* interest is more
fundamental than *my own* interest. This is bedrock. This is why Alexander Schmemann claims that "feasts belong to the very deepest,
most primitive layer of human life and culture . . .; what remains constant is the need to celebrate."[26] This is also why the poor, the lame,
the widow, and all the marginalized come to the wedding feast before
the rich and respectable (Luke 14:5–24; cf. Matt. 22:1–14); they see
clearly that what counts finally is being at Jesus' huge, round dinner
table. This transforms us; it enables us to see that deepest delight—to
share—and that to share is to experience the delight of wholeness
with self, others, and all creation.

Learning to Feast and Celebrate

I don't think we can celebrate on command. It is probably almost
as difficult to feast authentically. Feasting is *not* a matter of eating
and drinking lavishly; one can overeat and overdrink by oneself in
obsessive self-indulgence that, from the outside, looks very much like
feasting. Nothing could be further from feasting, however. Feasting
is a good example of the fact that Christian practices are not only
observable external activities; they are also attitude- and disposition-

filled actions. It therefore only makes sense to approach this practice both by thinking about it and also by beginning to act our way into celebrating. We can learn how to celebrate and to feast, but that will take some doing.

Celebration in feasting is certainly more—much more—than only a matter for thinking. If we are about the business of learning how to feast, then we need to do more than reflect on this (as I did in the previous section of this chapter), important as that is. It would be ideal if we could experience feasting. Here I offer some suggestions for visceral experience.

1. The first step in learning how to celebrate is simply to focus our thinking on feasting for a while. When do you experience joy? Name a time when you can remember feeling joyous. Did you celebrate that occasion? What led you to celebrate?

    These reminders are good starting points for discussion of celebrations:

    *   Celebration is a corporate activity.
    *   We need to trust in God to dispel some of our anxiety and bring out our capacity for spontaneous enjoyment.
    *   Celebrations are generous, other-directed occasions.
    *   How do we benefit from a consciousness of the wonder of others, food, and interaction?
    *   Look for little moments of joy, of transformation, and for offering your whole life over to God.
    *   Dance whenever possible.
    *   Affirm celebration with love.
    *   Remember the role of silent meditation in celebration.

2. Do you think that we *need* to celebrate, as Alexander Schmemann affirms? Why might that be? How are feasting and community related to each other?

3. How does living the Christian life issue in celebration and lead to gaiety? Individuals can do the following things to increase their capacity to celebrate:

- simply relax
- find a pleasurable activity
- find a place to play
- watch a funny movie
- be mindful of the food you eat, chewing slowly and savoring
- try something new or frivolous; explore
- share these activities with a friend, getting together for relaxation and pleasure
- choose a person who seems to have a "spirit of carefree celebration," and ask him or her to discuss this with you. How does that person find joy in the midst of his or her struggles? What encourages his or her spirit?

4. It is no wonder that movies and television dramas have continued to remain a staple of our society; they allow people to vicariously experience all sorts of human activity. As we watch, we can begin to imagine ourselves into learning what all is involved in eating and feasting. Several movies—*Chocolat*; *Like Water for Chocolate* (do you see a pattern already?); *Big Night*; and *Woman on Top*—are enjoyable. My favorite is still *Babette's Feast*. I had thought everyone had seen this; imagine my surprise when no one in my Theology of Eating class had. Well, they loved it!

An excellent activity involving feasting in community is to show the film *Babette's Feast* or one of the others mentioned. This can be viewed by yourself, but it is more fun and more celebrative to see it with others. The film could be shown in two sessions, comparing feelings after the first hour with feelings

after the entire film. There follow some questions keyed to
Babette's Feast, but these are easily adapted to other films as well.

- What sort of reaction do you find yourself having to the
  Danish Lutheran religious sect?
- How is Babette different from the two sisters?
- Why did Babette make the feast that she did?
- How did the feast transform the group? Was it something
  in the nature of the feast?
- Which is your life closer to—the sect's ethos, or
  Babette's?
- Do you feel celebrative? Do you ever just let go and
  allow yourself to express joy? When? Are those times
  limited? *Why?*

5. Another visceral, holistic activity associated with feasting and
celebrating is music—singing together, playing together, or
listening together. Singing loudly is one way of letting go.
Feasting shares this quality of "letting go," of spontaneity.
Concoct an activity of joyous singing, which can be either
rousing church hymns or other popular tunes. It doesn't matter
how off-key.

6. When we share with others in celebration, we are contributing
to their sense of well-being. This fosters expansive growth,
emotional abundance, and openness for all involved. If we
believe that God is potentially or really present everywhere, how
could that impact our feasting? The capacity to celebrate taps
into the presence of God for many people.

   Plan a celebration with a small group of others. Ask God
to enable you to welcome others and to prepare an inviting
beginning. Trust that God can free you and others from anxiety.

   Have a dinner party to celebrate people getting to know
each other better—as acquaintances and friends or even as

strangers getting to know each other. Richard Foster and Kathryn Yanni have a number of good suggestions.[27]

7. Plan new and creative ways to celebrate an occasion in the life of a friend, especially occasions not ordinarily celebrated. Ask people to bring their favorite dish and tell a story about its creation or how it came to be in their eating repertoire. You could tie this in with the communion of saints. If a now-deceased saint of the local congregation used to always bring lemon meringue pie, bring such a pie, and commune with the saints in a number of ways!

8. Plan a meal using only local foods or only foods grown in the United States. Be creative.

9. How can we enrich occasions that are already celebrations of feasting, such as Thanksgiving, Christmas, Easter, and family holidays?[28]

FIVE

Preparing Food: The Forgotten Practice

MY FRIEND DAVE is pastor of a historic Presbyterian church in the heart of a small city in Kansas. He is doing great ministry there. This story is one that makes me proud to call him my friend.

When David got to this city he found that a majority of the population was Latino; besides longer-term settlers, immigrants had come to work in the meatpacking industry. The church had been basically oblivious to this fact. There was and is a great deal of poverty in the city; many people were going hungry, and some were homeless. David and a few other folks in town saw that there was a need to feed the hungry. Slowly at first they began to open the Presbyterian church to feed some people. After all, the church has commercial grade ovens that were being used at most only once a week. As time passed, more and more people got involved in feeding the hungry and more and more people started coming to receive a meal. Some of those who were preparing food also began to eat with those who were hungry.

Amazingly, last year the church fed 22,000 people out of its kitchen! This year Dave has been teaching Spanish to a number of people in the church and also introducing the Spanish language gradually into the church service by using Spanish for one element of the service at a time (Lord's Prayer, Apostles' Creed, call to worship, etc.). The group that prepares meals together has become a unit, and the church itself is becoming a more vital part of the community. Preparing food for the hungry has become an engine of revitalization.

Preparing Food as a Historic, Biblical Practice

Perhaps it was a male perspective that made me overlook the practice of preparing food at first. Much argues for its inclusion as a biblically based Christian practice. Part of sharing and hospitality and feasting (and of many of the other practices, like the Eucharist) involves the process of preparing food to be served or working together to prepare a meal for all those gathered.[1]

So why is preparing food overlooked? Why is it not as prominent as, say, fasting or saying grace? Why do you suppose we have so few accounts of Jesus preparing food in the Gospels? Who do you think prepared the Passover meal for Jesus that became the model for the celebration of the Lord's Supper? My thought (and I am sure it is one shared by thousands of women) is that the Gospel writers were men. They probably did very little preparation of food themselves. There are at least two indications of this. First, in Luke 10:38–42 Martha is made to appear in a bad light when she asks Mary to help her in the kitchen rather than continue conversing with Jesus. Then, at the feeding of the five thousand in Mark 6:37 (=Matt. 14:16; Luke 9:13), the disciples appear stunned when Jesus tells them, "You give them something to eat." How would they go about preparing food at all, much less that much?

Another reason may have to do with the fact that there were so many regulations concerning the preparation of food in the Hebrew Scriptures; read through Leviticus or Numbers sometimes. To differentiate themselves from Judaism, the Gospel writers may have dropped mention of dietary practices or of cooking food in the Hebraic custom. Certainly Jesus grew up practicing the dietary regulations. And certainly, I would want to claim that the sheer quantity of dietary regulations were important ways of worshiping God and acknowledging the source of those laws. Leon Kass argues that they were ways of sanctifying food and giving praise to God.[2]

Jesus himself prepares food on several occasions in the Gospels. For example, Jesus prepares breakfast on one occasion (John 21:9–14), and famously prepares wine (John 2:1–11), as well as feeding thousands and breaking bread at Emmaus (Luke 24:30). Paul has several discourses about how to prepare and serve food—what should and should not be on the menu, and how Christians are to practice table manners (Rom. 14:13–23; 1 Cor. 8:1–13; 11:17–34). Furthermore, we are told that the early Christians had all things in common and frequently broke bread together (Acts 2:43–47). How do you suppose that food got prepared?

Sharing the Preparing of Food

Patti and I used to have Judith and Stephen Shepherd over every other week. They had us over on the alternate weeks. I remember the time Patti and I used to spend getting food ready as fairly much fun but not a time I focused on. When Stephen and Judith got to our house, usually there was still a little left to do and all four of us did it together. When we got to their house, we did likewise. There was an intimacy to fixing food together, an energy that was less than explicit or recognized but that stays with me still.

That's how it is with my family. My son Robert is something of a chef, interested in cooking, always willing to try new things, and with a good sense of what might add to the taste of a particular dish. He is not much on cleaning up. However, when Robert and our little clan get together, we are each developing our own place in preparation. We wait on Robert to bring creativity and verve. Patti and I are the food gatherers and "sous-chefs." Nathan is the gofer—so far anyway. Heidi, Cara, and Michael are beginning to take on the clean-up. There is, if you will, a bit of a dance to preparing food, so that each of us knows our place and contributes our gifts. I mention this to indicate the mundane sorts of things that go into preparing and cleaning up and also to hint that those routines might contribute to our bonding and enjoyment. I need to add also that sometimes when we go to a lot of trouble preparing food the response of a family can be underwhelming.

Jane Goodall, author of *Harvest for Hope*, remembers her family's kitchen table with its companionship and conversation and fun and looks back on the meals of her childhood with nostalgia. Big family affairs, they were fun times to gather and share talk of the day and tease. There have been staggering changes since then, Goodall notes. "So many children are raised in households where all the adult family members work—from choice or from economic necessity—and no longer have the time or inclination to spend the hours in the kitchen preparing the kind of meals I enjoyed as a child."[3] The impact of preparing food and eating together goes beyond nutrition; children who eat meals with their families tend to do better in school and have fewer behavioral problems and less chance of substance abuse and depression later on in life.[4]

Perhaps when eating was a more direct matter of survival, the tribe would have been more invested in the process of hunting and gathering food. The whole group might have pursued their next meal more vigorously. Indeed, when that was the case (it still is in some societies), the family was more than an emotional haven. Perhaps it would be better to say that the emotions that were in play included bodily well-being as an aspect of family practice.

What emerges as being significant about preparing food together (rather than Mom doing all the work) is the mutuality that is being expressed in the process. This process exhibits the care taken over the quality of the dishes produced and hence a caring for each other. Clearly the process of cleaning up after the meal is part of this caretaking.

A gender issue lurks not far beneath the surface here. Women have typically done the preparation and cleanup for meals. That has changed; when it became clear that putting food on the table and cleaning up afterward were not seen as "real work" or were discounted in other ways, women just said, "Do it yourself." And in fact, the culture in general has done just this. The rapid increase in eating out and ready-to-heat takeout meals is testimony to this revolution. What has been lost thereby is not clearly visible.[5]

There is a contrasting example that is instructive and may begin to show us the value of preparation. At many family gatherings, on special occasions, or after a potluck at a church, women may still be seen washing up. During those times or during preparation time, real bonding takes place among women. Extended relatives, friends, and acquaintances find themselves talking about all sorts of things during that time. Cooking, washing dishes, complaining, making jokes about their partners, and sharing ideas and gossip are all part of this bonding. Men may do some of this around the barbecue grill, of course.

Preparing and Hospitality

There is a difference between preparing food for family and friends and preparing food for the homeless and hungry. Both are forms of sharing, to be sure. Hospitality, however, consists of participating together in directing one's efforts outward rather than inward. Participating together in both cases is terribly important, but the object or goal of one's efforts is different. With hospitality there is not a familiar or necessarily ongoing relationship with the others; they are often strangers or may even be enemies. While not assuming that everyone has the same motive in either sharing or hospitality, both the product and the process are different in the two cases.[6]

Think back to the story of Dave and the Kansas church. There the effort began with a few people who saw a need and began to address it. The food kitchen was designed to be a friendly and open place with as little manipulation as possible. What happened in the course of preparing and serving meals was that the preparers discovered that hospitality met a need in themselves as well as for those who were hungry. Relationships developed among the preparers and also among those being served. Hospitality began to blur the distinctness of the line between the servers and the served. Mutuality developed with the caretaking. There came to be a "family atmosphere" even though it would be wrong, I think, to confuse family with the food kitchen.

Those who did the preparing generated their own set of dynamics, however. Bonding emerged in the group that was serving and preparing the meals. Ongoing relationships were created among people who were members of the church and also those in the community who were participating, both as servers and as served. While I do not want to romanticize this project as though it were the kingdom come, it does share some elements of Jesus' table fellowship. It makes me think as well of Jesus' footwashing action (John 13:1–20). Some churches see this activity as a sacrament or at least a sacramental.

Preparing Food for Feasting

Exacerbating the decline of feasting (and probably contributing to it) is the sheer quantity of things we feel we "have to do" to enjoy a satisfying life. Time is short, and when we eat, we frequently just "grab something." We do not take time to prepare food. My claim here is that preparation is one of the elements that goes into feasting, and if we cannot or do not take the time to prepare, we cannot feast. In some ways this has to do with how much time we have for one other (or, in fact, for ourselves, since preparing food can be a deeply satisfying experience). It is perhaps unrealistic to assume that we could prepare careful meals three times a day; most families are two-income earners and simply do not have the time. But if we do not take time to prepare any meals carefully we avoid exhibiting care and fail to learn mutuality by so doing. Preparing meals can seem a real burden unless we have the time to do it well. However, if we have the time and include others in the preparation, it can be a wonderful time.

The process of preparation and the anticipation of the feast are as much parts of the practice as the feast itself.[7]

Preparing for the Eucharist

Another practice in which preparation of food is involved is that of the Eucharist. It is reported, "When they were eating, he [Jesus] took a loaf of bread and, after blessing it, broke it, [and] gave it to them" (Mark 14:22; cf. Matt. 26:26; Luke 22:19). Jesus was involved, in at least a minimal way, in preparing food. Somehow the bread and wine (or grape juice) got to the table then, and it gets to the table now. (Imagine what might happen if there were no bread and wine at a sacramental celebration!) Someone either buys or makes the bread and probably buys Communion wine (though Wartburg Seminary always makes its own; see the following paragraph). In the *anawin* Roman Catholic community in Dubuque where my family worshiped, a different person baked the Communion bread each week. I remember still—my taste buds seem to remember—the taste of those chunks of whole wheat and honey bread. The body of Christ indeed. With a little imagination, one could believe that this was the "bread of life." The care and work that went into that Communion bread and the knowledge that one of us had baked the bread contributed to its taste. Baked in a circle, it was striated in concentric circles, and thus one broke off an interconnected part, a chunk, of the whole.

At Wartburg Seminary in Dubuque, Iowa, Frank Benz and then Ron Schardt cultivated a small vineyard behind the seminary buildings. Just beyond the parking lot where everyone could see it all year long, the vineyard produced a harvest of grapes once a year. Students and faculty worked together to gather the grapes, and the wine master oversaw the activity. The wine was decanted into Castle Wine, the brand name for Wartburg, and was then used for the Communion wine every Wednesday. Sometimes bottles of it were given as gifts to visitors, but those were the only two uses that were made of the wine. It was significant to know that the produce that eventuated in the blood of Christ had been grown in our own backyard.

Winemaking itself got a great impetus from the monasteries of Europe where the monks would make wine for Communion. Historically this was where the great vineyards—at least of the Western world—had their start. The wheat that became Communion bread no doubt was local wheat that had been gathered and prepared and cooked before it found its way to the table. The Roman Catholic Mass still incorporates the line, "Through your goodness we have this bread to offer, which earth has given and human hands have made . . . ; wine to offer, fruit of the vine and work of human hands."[8] This line suggests to me that in some ways the Creator is also the Preparer. This becomes particularly poignant if one considers God also as Mother.

So preparation was involved in the practice of Eucharist where local bread and wine were shared among the believers. Someone still sees to it that bread and wine arrive at the table. Usually, though, the process of preparation is quite private and seen at best as "deacon's work" or the work of the "altar guild."

Other Practices

Elements of food preparation are incorporated also into other practices. Fasting often begins with a small meal and also is broken in the same way. Some of those who fast prepare that food with an awareness of how good it will taste upon breaking the fast. Eating slowly and appreciatively is a good way to break the fast appropriately; it adds to the sense of the goodness of the gifts of food that God gives us.

In honoring the body, Christians have practiced an asceticism that recognizes how vital are the selection and preparation of healthy, nutritious, and nonfattening foods. How one goes about preparing food can be an individual dieting regime, and it can be far more fun if done with others.

Christian Features of Preparing Food

Four features of preparing food are distinctively Christian in character: service to others, mutuality, caretaking, and submission to others.

1. *Service*. One of the ideals of the Christian faith is service to others. This clearly derives from the command to love the neighbor as oneself. In our culture, however, service to others is not highly valued. Preparing food, in our culture, has come to be seen as service to others. To many persons the word "service" conjures up images of servants, silver service, room service at a hotel, service station, and the food service at colleges—all of which are viewed as of modest importance. There is some little irony in the fact that being of service to others is generally held in low esteem.

However, there is another understanding of service, and that is of being of service to others, an aspect of Martin Luther's understanding of vocation. For Luther the basic function and common feature of a vocation from God was the mediation of God's grace to others. Furthermore, for Luther, how one carried out one's vocation—its style—was important as well. For him and for John Calvin and other theologians, one's work could be a vocation, a calling from God, no matter how high or low the esteem in which the culture regarded it; this includes, for example, homemaking, cooking, dishwashing, and other aspects of food preparation.

Both sharing and hospitality are obviously means of service. Relieving the hunger of others stands alongside clothing the naked, sheltering the homeless, and visiting prisoners as important Christian ministries.

2. *Mutuality*. Several times in the New Testament Christians are exhorted to maintain a bond of mutual love among themselves. Preparing food together is one way of being mutually supportive and enjoying fellowship. Now the preparation of food has often been seen as a matter of self-sacrifice, as have the activities of making a home for one's partner and children, which was often seen as "women's work." Indeed, the recent theological battles about self-sacrifice

have revolved around the fact that women were consigned by culture and custom to make sacrifices. This has given homemaking (and the preparation of food in the home until recently) low status.

It was not the preparation of food itself, however, that has been seen as lesser in status, but the demeaning way that women were treated and the drudgery that often passed for "self-sacrifice" (which, of course, was not "self" sacrifice at all). But preparing food is now in vogue, and great chefs are coming into their own. Even food preparation in the household, if it is open to both women and men and voluntarily adopted, has become popular. One of the Christian features of this is the mutuality that it engenders. The ideal is that of equality in relationships and a mutuality of effort.

3. *Caretaking.* Taking care of others has also been associated with women. To find negative connotations in this would violate Christian values. Jesus counseled his disciples to serve each other and all people. Indeed, he himself set the example by washing the feet of the disciples (John 13).

4. *Submission to others.* This is surely one of the most counter-cultural and difficult of Christian practices.[9] Its basic thrust is that it is wise for us sometimes to submit to others' plans and intentions. We do not always have to have our own way. It is an act not only of humility but also of wisdom to listen to others and to follow their lead. God operates through others as well as through us. In terms of preparing food, submission to others involves learning from others, taking their preferences and dietary needs into account, and being willing to be a good host or hostess. Hosting itself is an act of submission that involves putting others' convenience and enjoyment first.

Learning to Prepare Food

How ridiculous! We think that everyone knows how to prepare food. I can assure you, however, that many divorced men, who all of a sudden have to fix their own meals, do not have this skill. This is true in many other cases as well. Here I raise questions and offer activities by which you can begin to ferret out what is involved in preparing food and how valuable a practice that might be.

1. Think back to a time when you prepared food with others, either at home or at a friend's house or at a soup kitchen. What do you remember? What do you think was added by preparing food with others?

2. Is there something about the fact that your bodies are involved in working together to prepare food that produces an intimacy among those who are doing so? Is *intimacy* the right word?

3. Sometimes when I am cooking, I think of myself as a maid or kitchen servant. This often happens when I am washing mushrooms, cutting celery or carrots, or arranging food on trays. I have to remember that I chose to do this. How do you imagine that I could get past this sense that I am demeaning myself by doing this? How could you?

4. Usually the process of preparing bread and wine for Communion is done privately by one or two "deacons" or members of the altar guild. What alternatives are there that would reflect the fact that it is the whole congregation that needs to (or gets to) prepare for Communion?

5. A number of EarthSchool curricula offer students the opportunity to learn how to track food from being a seed or baby animal through the process of growth and into preparation for a meal. Why do you think these are becoming popular?

6. Have you noticed that a number of institutions now offer cooking classes? Or that cookbooks are all the rage (not that they ever went out of fashion, but their numbers seem to be

increasing)? What does this mean? Why are they popular? Does the answer here seem to fit with your answer to question 4 above?

7. One thing we like to do at our house is to prepare at least one meal a week (yes, sometimes only one) with care, trying out new dishes and having others over to enjoy them with us. You might want to subscribe to a food magazine like *Food and Drink*, *Bon Appetit*, or *Gourmet*, or just read your newspaper carefully to find a new dish, or try out a family recipe. Carve out enough time to do it right, fix it together, and enjoy!

8. Volunteer to help prepare (and, if possible, serve) food in a soup kitchen or mission or Catholic (or Protestant or ecumenical) Worker house. Many churches offer a dinner meal once a week to those who need to have meals.

SIX

Fasting for Life

FRANK AND MARTHA are both college graduates, and Frank also has a master's degree. They are a rather typical U.S. couple in that they have accumulated an enormous amount of debt—cars, credit cards, loans for vacations or home improvement.

Frank and Martha have been married five and a half years, have a two-year-old daughter, and are both currently employed. When their daughter was born, they bought a house to make sure they had a suitable place to raise her and also to take advantage of tax credits for homeowners. Since the birth of their daughter, they have been unable to save money. They regularly borrow money at fairly high interest rates to pay short-term bills, such as meeting their two car payments, vacation loans, and home improvements. Their small savings account is diminished, and they have accumulated more debt than they are comfortable with.

Like many Americans, they are "at high risk of financial disaster as U.S. society virtually requires two incomes to meet even modest financial obligations. . . . [They] could not rely on their assets to replace lost earnings if they were suddenly unemployed. . . . [They] are not accumulating assets to pay for potential future expenses such as college education for their children and a comfortable retirement."[1]

Frank and Martha, like many North Americans, did not seriously consider the possibility of not having a second car in order to avoid taking on more debt. The point is not to be judgmental but to emphasize that abstaining tends to be beyond our imagining today. Our society doesn't consider the possibility of voluntarily abstaining from buying or consuming or having things because of lack of money.

Although fasting usually refers to abstaining from food, it can refer to abstaining from anything. Some people abstain from television or drugs or alcohol or cell phones, or constant media stimulation or overpacked schedules. Fasting is voluntary abstinence, a positive practice. Here I will emphasize fasting from food for spiritual reasons—to get in touch with God and to see ourselves as we are.

At the conclusion of this chapter, I offer some practical guides to reflection and action in learning to fast. Of all traditional practices, fasting is the one that seems most at odds with the values of affluent cultures. Fasting seems like an antiquated idea to most of us; it is certainly countercultural. That may also be why it is valuable; it uncovers some of the discomfiting and self-destructive patterns we nevertheless cling to.

Fasting could be the most valuable spiritual practice for American churches in our time. This is perhaps a bold statement, but one that I defend in this chapter.

Up to this point in my look at eating practices, I have emphasized those that foster delight and celebration. We say grace and pray in gratitude to God for the bounty that we savor. We celebrate in feasting as a way of remembering the beauty of creation, the work of the Spirit, and the incarnation of Jesus Christ as the head of our community. Our sharing with others grows out of the experience of being shared with; our hospitality to others is itself an outpouring of the hospitality God has shown us.[2] Preparing food with others can be both fun and meaningful. Thus one might think that a theology of eating is joyful and that spiritual practices are only affirmations of the positive.

We know better. We have heard the cry of the poor, the starving, the baby sucking at breasts long dry, and the diseases that accompany malnutrition. Closer to home, we know the diseases of too much—

too much fat, too much sedentary work, too many heart attacks, too much diabetes, too many obese kids. Both eating and the lack of food to eat have ugly sides. Not everyone has food to say grace over. Not everyone can feast. Many have nothing to share. Others have trouble saying grace over food that comes at the expense of domestic or global farmers, land, farm workers, and food workers. Others eat too much and unwisely. Others hoard their great abundance. Still others seek to engineer *jouissance* and meaning by controlling all life on the planet.

Complicity and Lack of Enjoyment

Michael Pollan contends that Americans cannot enjoy their food. They have reduced food to its nutrient components and have forgotten how to eat.[3] I think he is right on the money, but he hasn't yet excavated the deeper reason for this. The surface reason is that we have too much and we eat too much. The deeper reason is, in a word, complicity—not guilt. We feel bad eating when we know that others are hungry. We want to avoid facing the indirect ways we are implicated in the hunger of the world. We benefit from others' hunger; we appropriate the benefits of the evil that is part of the disorder of the global food system.[4] If we call this "guilt," then our response takes two paths: one is simply to blow it off because we know we aren't so directly involved as to merit the label "guilt"; the other is to repress the feeling of responsibility altogether and to desensitize ourselves to the suffering of others. Eventually we just flat out ignore such feelings. I believe that complicity ignored has the impact of a nemesis that blinds us to the feelings of others, to our responsibility, and to the food we would like to enjoy with an easy conscience. Over time, it shapes our character and the persons we become. As we repress our feelings, we also blunt our capacity to enjoy.

The inability to come to an awareness of the millions of hungry and starving people in a world where there *is* enough for all, and the inability to become alert to our role in this is part of an even larger picture. These two inabilities are "negations" in the way that Douglas John Hall has used the word. His thesis is that North Americans subscribe to an "official religion of optimism," which makes us unable to squarely confront the negations of life—death, murder, divorce, children on drugs, war, poverty, world hunger. We repress these negations because official religion cannot deal with them. The middle class sees them as "exceptions" rather than part of the social reality that we as a society need to address.[5] Indeed, we could not cling to the illusion of control were we to face them squarely. I am suggesting that we cannot fully enjoy food because of these repressions. This is broader than not enjoying food. It is hard to delight in anything if we continually need to repress the negations that are preventing many of our joys.[6] Hall suggests that a theology of the cross *can* deal with suffering, pain, and death. There is a resurrection hope, but it goes through the cross. We Americans want our lives to be all resurrection and no cross.

A corollary to this dynamic is that we middle-class Christians and citizens have not had to deal much with negations. According to Esther Thomas, a pastor from Sierra Leone, our discomfort comes from having too much. We have not been able to imagine even discomfort, much less hunger or starvation. Maybe that is changing. The events of 9/11 and of Katrina brought vulnerability into view. I wonder whether there was a ballooning of people's eating and weight in the wake of these disasters. Maybe the experience of obesity, the false promises of consumerism, and environmental threats (for example, high gas prices) are bringing the less secure side of life into view. That may be an asset if we can face and deal with negations. It may even rebound to an increased capacity to enjoy (and also to share).

The Path of Confession

I hope that the events we have experienced recently have brought us to the brink of self-awareness and self-examination. If there is any benefit in the increased level of fear and vulnerability we experience, perhaps it is that of allowing us to come to a conscious awareness of negations. We can begin to lift the cover off the dark side of our lives and see how interactive our own style of life is with others. We can begin to see how our overconsumption comes at the (indirect) cost of others' malnutrition. Rather than repress this knowledge, pollute our own character, and limit further enjoyment, we may—with relief—be able to allow it to surface, acknowledge it, and act to ameliorate its intensity and our own desensitization.

According to the "official religion of optimism" (Hall), if you ignore the negations of life, they have no influence—indeed, they do not exist. Brought into the light of day, this is revealed as "magical thinking" and irrationality. There is a disjunction between our perception of reality and the negations we inevitably encounter. However, like all persistent myths, there is a half-truth underlying our blind optimism. If one's perception does not include the possibility of forgiveness and renewed life, then blind optimism and magic may seem a better choice than despair.

Christians believe in a different proclamation, one of whose central features is precisely God's promise of forgiveness and renewed life. We believe that such forgiveness and renewal must travel through confession and repentance. For many people in our culture, confession and repentance appear depressing, a matter of despair or negative thinking. Christians believe that only by trusting in God's steadfast love can we find the profound strength we desperately need to forgive others and most of all ourselves. Only in this way can we find the healing and restoration that can generate new life. As Marjorie Thompson puts it, "Self-examination and confession do not call us to self-hatred or self-condemnation; they open the door of our heart to cleansing, renewal, and peace."[7]

Self-examination and confession are linked to spiritual practices based on a belief in God's inalienable, unconditional love. Only on the basis of that belief can we be realistic about our own brokenness and sin and thereby be led to honest confession. Because we recognize that grace stands at the center of our lives, we see ourselves as dependent on God to forgive us and to strengthen us for Christian life. This enables us to face the truths of reality.

We know that genuine confession before God and one another is the ground for authentic reconciliation and transformed living. The purpose of confession is an act of worship. Enabled by grace and convicted of our brokenness, we confess to God that we want to change, that we want to live with compassion and love of neighbor. "It is precisely because we are worth so much in God's eyes," writes Thompson, "and ought so to value one another and ourselves, that we confess our shortcomings."

> We place our hope in God's forgiveness and renewal, trusting that changeable attitudes and behaviors do not indelibly define who we are. A true spirit of confession actually increases authentic self-acceptance and love.[8]

Furthermore, and of utmost importance for this topic, is the reality that through confession and repentance we gain a sense of our complicity in the common human condition of sin. That makes the forgiveness of others possible. "As we see our weaknesses released and healed by a gracious God, we become capable of sharing the gift with others. God's freely offered love softens our hearts, so that we can free others. . . . Such forgiveness is the ground of reconciliation . . . and peacemaking."[9] It is also the motivation for remedying our complicity in others' suffering.

Before discussing the first four eating practices (chapters 2–5, above), I established their foundation as grateful responses to all that God has done for us. Before examining the next two eating practices, fasting and honoring our bodies (in this chapter and the next), I emphasize the response of repentance, confession, and transformation. This response is certainly not sealed off from that of gratitude. Instead, our gratitude to God both necessitates and enables confession as the path to new life.

This practice of self-examination and confession more naturally precedes consideration of fasting and honoring our bodies. These two are more ambivalent than the first four. This is to say that fasting and caring for our bodies are practices that stem from a recognition of our sinfulness. At the same time, it is vital to recognize that the possibility of transformation results from the ability to confess and repent that grace makes real. This enables us to work for justice.

The motive for fasting arises out of a hunger for God's direction in our lives. Prayer always accompanies fasting, both historically and in my experience. Fasting responds to our appetite for God's priorities, which themselves correspond to the deepest yearnings of our hearts. We want more of God's presence; we seek the counsel of the Spirit; we follow Jesus' own example of fasting to discern the will of his Father. Fasting drives us to penitence, and through penitence to confession and transformation. Transformation leads us to a quenching of our thirst, to wholeness.

Through fasting we examine our lives. Fasting enables us to come to an awareness of ourselves standing in front of God; it also enhances our insights and enables us to deal with whatever life brings—even our deepest flaws and shortcomings, life's negations. God loves to give to us. God gives us the Bread of Life, which a fast-induced hunger leaves us ready to receive.

We are not going to defeat the empire on its own terms. We have to pray for God's healing of all peoples and nations. We have to embody and live out the kingdom. Fasting is one way to do that.

Fasting

The practice of fasting has a long and venerable history, from the early Israelites to Jesus to Christian history. At the outset of this chapter, I claimed that fasting could be the most valuable spiritual practice also for us. It is now time to make good on that claim. I base this claim on two aspects of our current situation, the disease of overconsumption and our complicity. Fasting from food addresses both of those imprisoning realities.

To be sure, Martin Luther, John Calvin, John Wesley, and Jonathan Edwards all commended and practiced fasting. Two of the reasons Calvin commended fasting are related to its peculiar relevance and popularity. Calvin recommended fasting (1) to subdue the needless desires of "the flesh" and (2) to express humility before God in confession.[10] Actually, Calvin added a third: "to prepare for prayer and meditation," which can be linked to either of the other two. John Wesley was also committed to this practice. He asked, "Is not the neglect of this plain duty (I mean fasting, ranked by our Lord with almsgiving and prayer) one general occasion of deadness among Christians?"[11]

There are two aspects of the curative power of fasting. The first has to do with coming to an awareness of our limits and hence our dependence on God. The second has to do with a sense of penitence and desire for transformation so as to counteract our complicity in the evil of world hunger.

Combating Overconsumption and Coming to Know God and Ourselves

One of the most demonic aspects of our affluent culture is that it has blinded us to what is enough. We have learned that there is no such thing as *over*consumption; indeed, at times we are instructed that our patriotic duty is to consume. But there is no end to that. We know that no quantity or quality of automobiles, food, lifestyle, family, or home is finally going to be enough to satisfy the gnawing sensation inside us.

Our economy appears to be giving us all that we need. Indeed, our industries and our politicians try to persuade us that this is so. Yet, for some reason we feel dissatisfied. The bounty that we have is not enough—and will never be enough. John Mogabgab reports that in the average U.S. household the television is on seven hours a day. Viewing so much advertising generates discontent and encourages us to consume away that discontent. Furthermore, he writes, "Across a lifetime the average adult in the U.S. will eat the meat of seven 1,100 pound beef cattle. Ingestion of goods and services has become nothing less than the way to achieve economic and social health."[12] Virtually anything can be processed into a consumable to satisfy our appetite for pleasure or entertainment. "Have it your way" is the mantra of the marketplace. Can we have it our way without the risk of forgetting God's way? Can we hunger for Christ, the Bread of Life, when we are full of dishes enticingly served up on the steam table of contemporary culture?[13]

Despite most people's greater fear—the fear of scarcity—there is also a problem with too much. When there is too much, we no longer know what our limits are or what our dependencies are. We imagine that we are limitless, but we know that the maintenance of the illusion of control requires that we ignore negations and our own boundaries. We are stuck between self-delusion and despair. Fasting is a way through those two pathologies.

Marilyn Chandler McEntyre brings us up short with her striking comment: "[I]n a culture driven by endless cries of 'More!' fasting can simply be a faithful affirmation of 'Enough.'"[14] To be hungry during a fast is to know something of bodily need: it is to be reminded of our continuous need for food; it is to know that we are dependent rather than being in control. Fasting counteracts consumption; it is a radical act of abstinence from food. It is a stand against consumption best shared with other Christians. It is an act of resistance and self-affirmation. Mark Buchanan suggests that fasting is also a response to the leading of God. "Fasting begins in a hunger for more of God's direction in life. Fasting is honing an appetite for more of God's presence, wanting God to lead, waiting for the Spirit to drive."[15]

Fasting is often motivated by a desire to examine oneself before God, to get in touch with the spiritual reality of who one is, and to do penance. It is not motivated, as a diet is, primarily by desire to lose weight. (Dieting, however, can be a spiritual practice; see chapter 7, on honoring the body.) Nor is fasting an obsessive need to be slender or to be in control, as is often the case with eating disorders. Some people simply cannot fast for medical reasons.

One of the worst effects of overconsumption is that it fosters an ignorance about who we are. Particularly it hides the nature of our limits and the fact that we are finite, dependent beings. As we become increasingly hungry during a fast, we become aware that we are embodied creatures subject to the headaches, grouchiness, and a gnawing sensation that we may not recognize at first. If our fast continues for a day or two, our bodily responses may become more insistent. We may be humbled as to the range of our capabilities.

At the same time, amazingly enough, as we become viscerally aware of "the desires of the flesh" we may gain a clearer recognition of who we are. We can appreciate our priorities. It is as though the freedom from food enables us to see more clearly, to think more nimbly. We become aware of our dependency on food and other consumables and of how our over-consuming is killing us, both physically and spiritually. The disease attacks and shrivels our hearts.

Fasting can make us aware of our dependence on soil, water, farmers and farm workers, truckers, shelf stockers, checkout clerks, refrigerator technicians, and oven manufacturers. Hunger "opens our eyes and our guts to our own stark-naked neediness, our own daily dependence; that unless God in mercy provides food, manna, for this day, we're in trouble."[16] After only eighteen hours of not eating, we can become newly aware of our dependence on the Creator. We are that close to spiritual perceptiveness; our spiritual vision can snap back to 20/20 that quickly. Fasting enables many (but not all) to live in recognition of who we are and who God is. It rips off the blinders of overconsumption.

Gunilla Norris, in her article "Many Ways: Fasting toward Self-Simplification," expands the notion of fasting and includes fasting from consumerism, from complexity, from hurriedness, and from First World privilege. Her perspective is that we need to fast from that which does not genuinely feed us. Even one day of self-simplification (fasting from food)

> brings me to my knees. I see how much I have moved away from dependence on God's presence, how much I need to feed on forgiveness and mercy, how meaningless and tiring my self-appointed importance has become. I need to rest from my false notion that I can nourish myself and so be more open to be fed by God.[17]

Norris's point is that we fill ourselves up with that "which does not satisfy" (Isa. 55:2). Fasting is one way of allowing God to determine our worth and to let God's love be the ultimate foundation of our lives. If fasting is a small death, it can also show us our vulnerability and push us to turn to the Bread of Life. Our fear and insecurity can becomes less pervasive. Instead, fasting offers us the possibility of being empty enough to experience being filled with God's love. Then we may be centered enough to move into a rich, voluntary, and focused simplicity.[18] Practiced continually, fasting enriches the experience of being filled up.

Complicity, Penitence, and Wholeness

This brings us to the second reason why I claim that fasting is a central spiritual practice for our time. It addresses complicity. We know that our lifestyle is bought at the expense of others' suffering and even death. We know that we live off the fat of the planet even as others live from day to day. In the first ten hours of 2004 (and every year thereafter), we in the U.S. spent as much on our own weapons systems and other aspects of defense as we will pay the entire rest of the year for agricultural programs addressing long-term needs of the hungry in the poorest regions of the earth.[19]

Complicity is not the same as primary responsibility (when we do not meet our responsibilities, we rightly feel guilty). But we are often, and understandably, overwhelmed by the enormity of the issue of world hunger and our own powerlessness. We recognize our part in the problem. How can we live with integrity as rich Christians in an age of hunger? There is a way of combating the injustice of the material maldistribution into which we are born. There are ways of addressing our complicity. Our Christian integrity depends on practicing them.

Fasting Our Way
Past Overconsumption and Complicity

Most important is the realization that we do not have to solve all the problems of the world or "save the children" before lunch. We have just seen that fasting makes us aware of our limits, our dependence on God, and, in fact, on the love of God. This also means that we can accept our limited responsibility as a privilege. Let me spell that out a bit.[20]

1. Fasting enables us to get hungry enough to understand those who are perpetually hungry. We middle-class Americans rarely *ever* get hungry. My students from Liberia, Kenya, and Tanzania know what hunger is. They remind me of the Congolese children with skin-thin arms and bloated bellies among whom I grew up as the child of missionaries. Fasting produces just enough urgency to remind me of their situation. When I find myself in front of the refrigerator (again!) and have to restrain myself from grabbing a bite, I am momentarily and fleetingly sympathetic for those without refrigerators.

That sensation of the common humanity I share with others humbles me. Without food we are, after all, only a few days away from starvation. Fasting evokes a visceral appreciation and casts a strobe light on the whimsy and providence of being born into the middle class. It also makes us aware of others' hunger and of our indirect responsibility for or complicity in their plight. Fasting brings us to our knees; it allows us to become aware.

2. Fasting enables us to be penitent. We become penitent not in the sense that we are directly responsible but because the political

and economic structures of the world benefit us to the detriment of others. Fasting makes us aware that we have done nothing to deserve our good fortune. By voluntarily abstaining from food, we come to taste the conditions that millions of God's children constantly endure. We take upon ourselves, for a moment, their involuntary deprivation. And we realize that we don't have to be stuffed; we may be in our spiritual peak condition when we fast. We may also realize that we live not by bread (and consumables) alone, but by every word of God. We may come as close as we can to seeing God. We learn what Jesus meant by saying, "Feed my sheep" (John 21:17).

In the face of such disparity we are penitent; we confess our undeserved advantage. We confess our complicity. In that moment we begin to experience relief that the truth is out, that our responsibility has been laid flatly on the table. We are able to see penitence as a step toward wholeness.

3. Penitence leads to confession and transformation. In penitence we confess our obsession with consuming and our studied blindness to undeserved privilege. We drop our pretense, which has become a burden, and can begin to live with reality. Confession is made possible only by grace.

Fasting also shows the way forward. It points toward transformation. Two verses, Isaiah 58:6–7, are still among the best in showing the connection between our fasting and the compassion for others that God seeks:

Is this not the fast I have chosen:
to loose the chains of injustice
    and untie the cords of the yoke,
to set the oppressed free
    and break every yoke?
Is it not to share our food with the hungry
    and to provide the poor wanderer with shelter—
when you see the naked, to clothe him,
and not to turn away from your own flesh and blood? (NIV)

Here the linkage between fasting, feeding the hungry, and one's own transformation toward wholeness is quite evident.

The primary issue is not saving the world or ending hunger, though for both we are to pray and work. It is to do the best we can, in light of God's will and in God's power, to love our neighbor as ourselves. If we do, we will address the hunger of the world—the spiritual as well as the physical hunger. If the poor of the world are facing physical illness and malnutrition, we, the affluent of the world, are facing spiritual illness and malnutrition. Our lack of sensitivity and awareness of our own need to be delivered from obsessive grasping and an unrealistic drive for security cripple us in many ways. The diseases are quite different, but we suffer from forces that numb and deaden us.

Perhaps overconsumption and complicity are symbiotic symptoms of our illness. We may consume as a way of meeting our needs for community and creative love. We may consume as a substitute for intimacy and meaning. Consumption may separate us from others, even as some go shopping to find community. But this is a poor substitute, and it leaves us seriously isolated. Complicity thrives in an individualistic ethos; it generates a level of guilt that immobilizes. It imagines that the only question is, "What can I do?" rather than, "What can we do?" It generates bystander behavior that fails to acknowledge legitimate involvement.

Fasting, by contrast, moves us toward, rather than away, from the other. It confronts us with the earth community, the web that is our home. We are fellow creatures with all that live, draw breath, feed, and feel. We are embodied members of the same species and share humanity with the human (and creaturehood along with the other-than-human) community. Our lives are only a scratch away from the chaos, tragedy, and starvation that afflict so many. To be aware of this, to confess our complicity before God, to repent and be open to transformation is nothing less than a conversion.

This can be a privilege. Fasting offers us the chance to come home to life in community, a community that is far deeper than the individualism we tout. It is a chance to realize wholeness with others. But all of this is predicated on the recognition of dependence, forgiveness, and being welcomed back to fullness. (Chapter 9 deals with the path of transformation, a path that all the practices help constitute and beckon us to travel.)

Learning to Fast

Because fasting is such a powerful practice, it is good to approach it with careful reflection and action. My experience is that fasting is best done with a group of other Christians. The purposes and terms of a fast need to be discussed. Furthermore, the group needs to ask God to bless their fast and to pray together that God will reveal what each (or all) of them needs to hear. (Of course, in order to hear, one needs to listen to God as well!) *Thus the first thing a group should do is pray.* The Christian practice of fasting is motivated by a desire to invite God into our lives more fully and to gain discernment into the way we live our Christian lives. We do that by emptying ourselves of distractions such as consuming.

1. Groups and individuals might want to think about the practice of fasting before beginning. Asking questions such as the following deepen the practice and help to surface those thoughts that have remained just below consciousness. Some questions:

    - What have been your experiences with fasting from certain foods or abstaining from alcohol or watching television, which are common Lenten practices?
    - What response do you have to the idea of fasting? What attracts you? What repels you?
    - How could people get closer to God during a time of fasting? Describe the difference between fasting that is centered on God and fasting that is not.[21]

An excellent strategy for arriving at and assimilating ideas is the Think-Pair-Share activity. First ask participants to silently think about the question(s) chosen for contemplation. (Persons may elect to jot down ideas. Make scratch paper available.) Next, each person selects a partner and they discuss their individual responses one-on-one. Then, it is time for whole group sharing. The discussion of the large group is much more meaningful and forthcoming if the opportunity for addressing the questions by oneself or with one other precedes the large group activity.

2. Answers to the initial questions could be discussed. Then each member of the group could decide to fast as she or he wishes, or the group could try to work out a common pattern (insofar as possible). At this point, the fasting begins. A second discussion phase, prayer, or activity is valuable in the middle of the fast. This provides reinforcement and encouragement. Similarly, at the end of the activity, a similar discussion of one or more of these questions is in order:

   • How do you feel? What sensations surprised you? Were there some uncomfortable or irritating feelings but also some pleasant ones? How was the experience of "emptying" yourself?
   • Did you have particular insights into your relationship with food, alcohol, television, or God? With Jesus?
   • Did it make any difference that you were sharing your fasting experience with others?
   • Do you believe that limits can be life giving? Would it be helpful to fast from something other than drinking or food? (Some examples are fasting from television, from passing judgment on yourself or others, from overscheduling, from shopping, from video games, or from any other potentially addictive behavior.)

- How would regular fasting and prayer change your relationship with God? How might it lead to repentance and transformation?
- Would fasting (or other abstinence) change your feelings about consumption in our culture?
- Might fasting lead to action in regard to those who cannot choose whether to eat or not (the hungry)?

3. Some practical suggestions about fasting can make the experience more meaningful.
   - Approach the practice intentionally. Set the parameters with the group (or by yourself) some time in advance so that the fast can be anticipated and God's help can be invited into the process to help focus thoughts.
   - Choose a time for the fast when you are relatively free from stress, physical exertion, or job pressures. For many this is not possible. Think about how to increase success in the face of stress.
   - Decide upon the nature of the fast. Will you only drink water? Only water and fruit juice? Abstain only from meat?
   - A very good way to get started is with a brief fast—say, from dinner one evening until lunch the next day. Subsequently, one could increase the fasting time from this initial eighteen hours to a longer period. (Remember that many people have already fasted in preparation for major surgery, so they have some experience.)
   - When you get a hunger attack, think about your reasons for fasting. The spiritual director at Wartburg Seminary, Ginger Anderson-Larson, suggests that the sensation of hunger could be seen as an invitation to pray during the fast.
   - Fast simply from a particular food so long as that fasting is an act of penitence, worship, and opening oneself to God's priorities.

- Consider donating the money you would have spent on food during the fast to a world-hunger agency or to a local organization that feeds the homeless and hungry.
- Don't isolate yourself from the fact that some people cannot fast because they have no access to food in the first place. Volunteer your help in assisting the foodless. Look hunger in the eye. In that way you may become empathetic with the sensations of those who are not abstaining voluntarily.
- Observe in yourself (and use a journal if that is useful) a sense of the good things you become aware of during your fast. Note your dependence on these blessings.
- When you break the fast, avoid the temptation to rush out and overeat or eat rapidly; it will not feel good. Respect what your body has to say.

4. There are many good resources on fasting. One might even say fasting is making a comeback. The books I particularly commend are:
   - Richard J. Foster, *Celebration of Discipline: The Path to Spiritual Growth* (San Francisco: Harper & Row, 1979, 1998), chapter 4.
   - Richard J. Foster and Kathryn A. Yanni, *Celebrating the Disciplines: A Journal Workbook to Accompany "Celebration of Discipline"* (San Francisco: Harper, 1992), especially pp. 17–21 and 96–102.
   - Marjorie J. Thompson, *Soul Feast: An Invitation to the Christian Spiritual Life* (Louisville: Westminster John Knox, 1995), chapter 5, and her notes on p. 152.

SEVEN

Honoring the Body

IT IS JUST NOT FAIR. Maybe four or five times a week I play racquetball and lift weights or walk or go bicycling or find some other way to exercise. I love to exercise. There are few things more fun than to take a hot shower after racquetball. Those little endorphins are running wild; it's easy to imagine myself as being more fit than any realistic estimate, and my whole body just feels alive. But does this translate into weight loss or the reduction of my waistline? It does not. It's just not fair.

How can this be? I suppose you know, if you have read this far, that I love eating. Sometimes it seems as though the food just teleports from the refrigerator or the pantry to my mouth—almonds, ice cream, fudge, you name it.

And then, I begin to think, maybe there's a connection. Right after Patti and I finish cycling in the summertime, most days we come in and fix a drink and then maybe a plate of nachos. We sit on the back deck, by ourselves or with neighbors, and we call this our "cruise." Pretty corny, but we love it.

So what's a person to do? How can I lose weight, keep up the exercising, and still love food?

We who are the affluent on today's globe struggle with knowing how much is enough. We don't know. In chapter 6, I examined a similar dynamic that leads to fasting and, through fasting, to forgiveness and renewal. I will follow the same path here, this time in regard to honoring our bodies.

Honoring our bodies may involve dieting and also fasting. Our bodies are the temples of the Holy Spirit, says Paul (1 Cor. 3:16). It is part of our calling from God to take care of our bodies, to respect them, and to enjoy their health and well-being. Honoring our bodies is a spiritual practice.

We are complicit in using more than our fair share of the earth's resources. However, when we do that, we find that we are *disadvantaged* by having too much. Saying that is not some verbal trick to induce guilt. There is such a thing as too much, and it is destructive. Most obviously, we find that we eat too much, and that not wisely.

Those of us who know this problem quite intimately know that this often feels like a curse. We simply do not know when to quit. We can't resist the cookie samples at the local grocery store, and we often find that a doughnut, a pizza, or almost anything sounds great. Like Winnie the Pooh, we are always ready "for a little something." Oh yes, we know about heart attacks, diabetes, snoring, respiratory disease, and the whole rest of the litany, but somehow. . . . When we overeat, our bodies remind us that we were putting food away so fast that we have (once again!) exceeded our stomach's comfortable carrying capacity. And that feels decidedly not good.

What about you? Are you comfortable with your body? Have you come to terms with it? Do you have the ability to practice a discipline that honors your body? Do you know when to say, "No thanks. I've had enough"? If so, I envy you.

It is instructive that I choose to begin a chapter on honoring the body with my battle with overeating. I could have begun with sex, which I also love, or with exercise, to which I am happily addicted. Instead, I begin with overeating. Why is that? Perhaps it is because we Americans have been socialized with all the diet industry admonishments in books, ads, food sales, and other media. We should be able to control our bodies, we think. The reduction of food to nutrients—carbs, fat, protein, cholesterol, sugars—make them a preoccupation that dampens enjoyment. Rather than attend to our eating mindfully in accord with bodily clues, we are obsessed with our weight. This obsession sets up a loss of enjoyment and a reactive overeating. In short, we see our bodies as a problem to be monitored rather than a gift. Instead of seeing our limits as enabling meaning and pleasure, we see our bodily limits as burdens to be superseded.[1]

There is a subtle dynamic here. We seem to be obsessing about maintaining discipline over our bodies, which actually undercuts our ability to discipline ourselves. In her book *French Women Don't Get Fat*, Mireille Guilano suggests why this is so.[2] She writes, "French women take pleasure in eating well, while American women see it as a conflict and obsess over it." Put differently, "French women typically think about good things to eat. American women typically worry about bad things to eat." Eating in North America has become "controversial behavior." Our obsession with weight is nothing less than a "psychosis" that adds stress "to our already stressful way of life," which is "fast erasing the simple value of pleasure."[3]

There is a sort of reverse discipline in operation. We suspect that the things that are pleasurable need to be disciplined for fear of their controlling us. An alternative strategy aims to discount pleasurable things. Discounting them may be just another way of controlling them. Our overdisciplining and overdiscounting deny pleasure, which is false. We do know how good a hot fudge sundae is. And so our attempts to diet (which is one discipline, some varieties of which are based on discounting and/or strict control) fail, as they must. A cynic might say we set them up to fail.[4] Our exaggerated estimate of our ability to control eating denies pleasure. And so we eat past satiety and wonder what happened. What evil demon made us eat the whole thing? Again.

The only way through this dilemma would acknowledge, indeed embrace, pleasure but find a framework that could limit overdoing. That is the framework that would answer the question of what is enough, too much, and too little. In short, we need a transcendent vision for honoring our bodies and enjoying them rather than fearing them or regarding them as potentially mutinous.

God and Eating

Sometimes our desire for comfort supersedes our discipline. On 9/11 the United States got a strong dose of its own vulnerability to attack. Hurricanes Katrina and Rita showed how little we can control nature. Those events raised the level of our insecurity and sense of fragility. I bet they led us to eat more. Some of us find comfort in food. We eat to overcome vulnerability and make us feel better. We may eat to fill ourselves up, a poor substitute for being whole. This is just the opposite of what those with other eating disorders do—they starve themselves to gain a measure of control and, according to Michelle Lelwica, to be made whole, or saved.[5] These issues of vulnerability, dependence, and longing to be made whole all suggest that eating and honoring the body are related to God. It is important to understand why honoring the body is a Christian practice. It is pleasing to God that we enjoy healthy bodies and take care of them. We are to be in touch with and celebrate our bodies as good creations. This applies to sex, exercise, and other physical activities as well as eating.

Our Christian faith is replete with beliefs that relate positively to the body. First, God created all that is—plants, animals, humankind, bodies all—and saw that they were good. God created food and bodies for pleasure, for delight. And they are good. This belief has been affirmed in our creeds, but we have sometimes not incorporated the goodness of food and our bodies into the way we live. Theology has often judged the body negatively no matter what we say. We simply don't believe that we were created in God's image.[6] Second, we believe in the incarnation of God in the human body of Jesus of Nazareth, who was born, ate, suffered, laughed, walked, and died. Jesus modeled a life of compassion, concern for bodily well-being, and inclusive fellowship. Scripture witnesses to Jesus' concern for the sick, the hungry, and the crippled, as well as to his frequent meals with his friends. The church, recognizing the interdependence of all its members, calls itself the body of Christ. A third major doctrine we confess is the bodily resurrection of Jesus and his ongoing presence with us through the power of the Holy Spirit. The resurrection of the body (our bodies!) certainly implies that bodies matter to God.

Eating is an activity that is integral to our bodily well-being, the honoring of our bodies. My claim is that God created food for bodily delight and for sharing. Stephanie Paulsell, in her eloquent book, *Honoring the Body*, gets the connection right:

> Is food our friend or our enemy? Is it a gift to be received with thankfulness or a problem to be mastered? It is not surprising that our questions about food are nearly identical to our questions about our bodies. For what other daily activity is more integral to the practice of honoring the body than eating and drinking? How we understand our bodies—as friend or as enemy, as gift or as problem, as sacred or repulsive, as temple of God's spirit or as a shell in which we are trapped—will influence how and what we eat and drink. How we eat and drink in turn, helps shape how we feel about our bodies and how those with whom we share our tables feel about theirs.[7]

If we recognize that our bodies are created by God for delight and sharing, then we will eat and drink in ways that honor our bodies. We will recognize that by doing this we are honoring God's intentions for them.

When we eat and drink in a way that honors our bodies—nourishes and delights us—then we are keeping our connection with the earth and with each other. Our bodies are vulnerable. We depend on the produce of the earth, on the respect and dignity that others accord us, and ultimately on the way God sustains and cares for us.

In eating, the vulnerability of our bodies is revealed. And yet we often eat to obscure our vulnerability, to forget our fears and frailty. This inconsistency can be explained as a feature of our upbringing in the United States (and other affluent countries). Born in a quite dependent relationship, we learn to be independent, to regard dependency as a flaw rather than a characteristic to be trusted. We equate dependency with immaturity. (This *may* be more true of men than women.) Rather than acknowledge and enjoy our interdependency, we deny this feature of our embodiment. One way we do this is to attempt to manage our bodies, to manage our eating, our appearance, our image, our personality. We are caught between denying our clear limitations and dependency and trying to manage what we can enjoy only by acknowledging our limits.

Trying to Control the Finally Noncontrollable

Denying our dependency involves dishonoring rather than honoring our bodies. We seek to deny vulnerability, to appear strong and self-reliant, to operate from a position of superiority. We dishonor our bodies when we seek to manage them as though they were foreign to us. This may be born out of a drive to deny our desires, to distrust them, to act as though they didn't exist. To desire is to be dependent on the object of desire. We delude ourselves. But if you examine the factors that go into healthy eating and healthy bodies, you realize that at most only some of them are under voluntary control. Yes, we should pay some attention to the amount of fat, carbohydrates, and proteins we eat; we should think about nutrition. What is out of balance is worrying to the point that we are out of touch with the sensuality and joy of our bodies.

I conclude that to honor our bodies means to respect them, to see them more as friend than enemy. To honor our bodies means that we trust them, not in such a way that we act on every impulse, but that we get in touch with who we are and what we are feeling. (I discuss how to do this in the concluding section below.)

I am impressed by the literature that claims that dieting may be counterproductive, that it in fact has—or at least can have—negative results overall.[8] This is because dieting assumes that one can control or manage one's body (and life, since the body is an integral part of one's life). Operating on this assumption produces a blindness about who one is. Acting with discontent and disrespect in the attempt to come to terms with one's body or at least gain some control over it is not the foundation on which a long-term honoring of one's body can be built.

Trusting Our Bodies

Honoring the body means to trust it. We need to see our bodies as enablements rather than as limiting factors or as appendages that need to be guarded against. Distrusting our bodies means that we need to manage them instead of appreciating them. Eating, then, becomes merely functional—a matter to be approached guardedly and out of necessity, not something we anticipate and relish. The image of our ideal body then involves a balance between easy acceptance and care.

Because eating and honoring our bodies are so closely interconnected, it is clear that the way we eat and the way we view our bodies are interconnected. Michael Pollan writes in an article titled "Our National Eating Disorder:"[9]

> Maybe what we should be talking about is an American paradox: that is, a notably unhealthy people obsessed by the idea of eating healthily. . . . Levenstein . . . neatly sums up the beliefs that have guided the American way of eating . . . "that taste is not a true guide to what should be eaten, that one should not simply eat what one enjoys; that the important components of food cannot be seen or tasted, but are discernible only in scientific laboratories; and that experimental science has produced rules of nutrition that will prevent illness and encourage longevity."[10]

To combat this paradox, Pollan writes, "The power of any orthodoxy resides in its ability not to seem like one, and, at least to a 1904 or 2004 genus American, these beliefs don't seem controversial or silly. The problem is, whatever their merits, this way of thinking about food is a recipe for deep confusion and anxiety about one of the central questions of life: What should we have for dinner?"[11]

Pollan's claim goes beyond what he realizes. The implication of his claim (since honoring the body and eating are interconnected) is that we have given over the honoring of our bodies to a set of scientific findings. We can no more appreciate our bodies than we can appreciate eating, if we have given over the dynamics that guide what constitutes healthy eating or healthy bodies over to some set of external principles. The tendency is to mistrust our sensations. If, on the other hand, we can find a way to honor the sensations of our bodies and of eating, then we can find a way to honor our bodies and our eating. That is my ultimate aim in this book. My second aim, that we may learn to share, rests on this first one. (I realize that many people have been helped by a strict diet, and I appreciate that. I do hope they can also enjoy the sensations of eating.)

The basic problem, that we have fallen out of touch with our bodies, is not irredeemable. This is a matter of degree. We cannot honor our bodies without seeing them as trustworthy, at least to some degree. If we do not delight in our bodies, then we must control or monitor them. That is what seems to be happening, exemplified with the diet of the month or the hot food fad of the year. If we have lost contact with our sensations, then it is difficult to imagine how we could honor them. We need to learn or relearn how to appreciate and how to come to terms with the goodness of our sensations. There are some who can teach us that. There are landmarks and examples about honoring bodies and eating enjoyably. Measuredness is part of that honoring.

In sum, we seem to be stuck in a double bind. On the one hand, we view our bodies suspiciously as entities to be managed, and thus we eat and drink with overattention to scientific and nutritional content. On the other hand, on a visceral level we view our bodies as vehicles of pleasure and learn to consume to please them and, frankly, sometimes we see eating and drinking as "the more, the merrier." There is a way past this double bind, and it involves changing our understanding of what constitutes health.

If the term *health* seems to have come out of nowhere, let me add this note: The matter of honoring our bodies is a practice that makes for health, if in fact it is not deeply part of our conception of health. How we eat and drink contributes to or detracts from our health. Thus, health is the wider goal and result of honoring our bodies.

Health as an Individual Project: A Misconception

In this culture we have so narrow a view of what counts for health that it would be good for us to expand it. Most citizens of affluent nations understand health as a commodity that is under our control, an individual property that we can manage. We believe that staying well is a matter of our own responsibility, that health is an individual concern. This view is compatible with a scientific management and functional understanding of the self.[12] Health is not seen as part of a system connected to the whole but rather as an atomistic, disconnected feature of the individual human's well-being.

To be sure, the individual body *does* have an integrity unto itself. However, this is balanced by the multiple ways the body is related to other people, the world of nature, and God. Our definition of health, with its emphasis on the individual integrity of the body, has become unbalanced. Thus, if we are to come to view the body as friend and as home rather than as an untrustworthy acquaintance or project, we need to expand our conception of health to include the ways the self is part of the earth community. Eating and drinking, as a part of the healthy honoring of the body, take on a different nuance in this wider perspective.

Our individualistic notion of health has fostered a commodification of our own and others' body concerns, things we believe we can manage. Rather than seeing health as a communal, mutual, and earth-related phenomenon, our scientific outlook has rendered health a project. There are any number of other factors that reinforce this view. Let me mention four.

First, most citizens are seldom really hungry in the United States. We have no bodily sensation of real hunger. Perhaps during a period of fasting we may feel the beginning of craving, but this is a voluntarily discipline. Without the experience of hunger, we can easily forget that we are protoplasmic material that requires sustenance from outside. We can forget our creatureliness and particularly our need for food and drink. The lack of hunger makes us believe that we can ignore food—its quality *and* how that food got to our tables. It renders food a constant that is taken for granted, as is the whole environment (air, soil, water, sun, seed) and human effort that entered into the Arby's cheddar melt we buy out of our car window. In contrast, understanding health as a relational activity reminds us that we hunger, and that hunger reveals our dependency on a widespread community beyond ourselves.

Second, seeing health as a product is consistent with a culture of consumption and individual acquisition. Many of us eat too much because we are socialized into buying and ingesting to generate bodily states—pleasure, joviality, intimacy of some degree, conviviality, friendship, etc. We also ingest pills to generate bodily states: the control of asthma, fertility, high blood pressure, cholesterol levels, depression, anxiety, insomnia, and vitamin deficiency.[13] There is a similarity in the way we buy and the way we eat to obtain emotional, mental, and physical sensations.

A corollary of this factor is, third, a tie-in with the "religion of success." What we eat and the sophistication of our tastes are one measure of success in affluent nations. Our notion of "eating well" goes far beyond sustainability and health. Sometimes we seem to eat as a token of status. We should earnestly ask whether these individualistic conceptions of health disguise the cost of our overconsumption to others on the planet. Rebecca Todd Peters asserts that "[r]ising standards of living for people in poverty are certainly a necessary part of addressing the social well-being of people, but continued rising standards of living for the global elite around the world are simply a reflection of greed and avarice."[14]

A final factor that feeds into seeing health as a project is our vulnerability and fear of the unknown. While this has become more intense in the past five years, it reinforces our drive for self-sufficiency and independence. We suppress from our consciousness our dependency on much in the world that is beyond our control. In that way we cut ourselves "off from a sense of the vulnerability of our bodies, which need nourishment to keep us breathing. We will be unable to learn what satisfies us. And we will live unconscious of the way God sustains our life."[15]

The operative conception of health that I see in our society is that bodily well-being is an individual scientific concern. The germ theory of illness, for example, can be interpreted individualistically. We are to protect ourselves against others' diseases and to control what enters our bodies in ways that suggest we are hermetically separable from them. Is it clear that this concept of health is unhealthy? I hope so. Sin is interwoven into the fabric of "first world" lifestyles of overconsumption, indifference to others, and greed. These are one with our definition of health, which is actually ill health. Not only are they killing other beings elsewhere; *they are killing us.* This is counterproductive for the affluent, and eating is the primary example. Number two is the economic, social, and environmental conditions of ill health that many rural farming communities are experiencing as a result of policies that keep food cheap and that have advantaged large corporate enterprises. The overconsumption that impoverishes others and degrades the environment makes us fat and unhealthy.[16]

Health as Thoroughly Relational

Let me suggest a revised understanding of health that begins by building on an understanding of the body as inevitably and thoroughly relational. David Abrams points to our dependence on air as a vivid way of making this case:

> We may acknowledge, intellectually, our body's reliance upon those plants and animals that we consume as nourishment, yet the civilized mind still feels itself somehow separate, autonomous, independent of the body and bodily nature in general. Only as we begin to notice and to experience, once again, our immersion in the invisible air do we start to realize what it is to be fully part of this world.[17]

Breathe deeply!

Our dependence on air, on water, on food, on each other, and on God is integral to health and bodily well-being. Acknowledging and living in support of all life is essential to honoring our individual bodies, which are only relatively individual. Our health depends on the health of others. Only for a time could we suppose the validity of "apartheid thinking" whereby one sector of life benefits at another's expense.[18] Indeed, all life is related. The quality of the air we breathe, the meat or fruit we eat, the chemical content of the water, the life-giving or life-destroying quality of our relationships with others—how could we not suppose that these were part of our health? Rebecca Todd Peters indicates the way a person's health and communal health are integral to each other. "Postcolonials recognize . . . a moral universe in which individual actions are understood to have communal effect—for good or ill—and in which the well-being of the community is taken into consideration before individual decisions are made."[19] How, in the wake of the December 26, 2004, tsunami or the August 29, 2005, chaos of Katrina, which killed thousands of people, can we overlook our embeddedness in nature? How can we ignore the way relief efforts promote the health of victims—and the way the blocking of such efforts threatens them?

The Christian vision emphasizes a holistic understanding of health. The reality of a *shalom* creation, in which all beings have a role to play in the well-being of each other, and the future goal of restoring such a *shalom* express a mutuality of interdependence. We are to strive for justice for all because all are God's beloved creatures. Honoring the body is a way to get in touch with God's goodness and the sustaining of life. Honoring the body, whatever our vocations, is a way of realizing the presence of God and of discipleship at work, at home, and wherever we are. Indeed, our hungers and our needs—like those of Jesus—point to our relationship with God. We learn thereby to cherish the body rather than to manage it.

Since the God who created bodies saw them as good, we should too. We should honor our bodies. We can trust them. Indeed, we honor God by honoring our bodies. Rather than listening to numerical counts of calories or carbs, we can listen to our bodies. We can be mindful of them.

Healthy, Honoring Practices

With a revised notion of health, our thoughts about a healthy order of eating change as well. Since honoring our bodies includes a concern for health as a goal, we have to shift our conception of health. For example, an understanding of health as an individual project leads to a rather narrow focus on nutritional content and temperance. By contrast, viewing health as a holistic state of relationships does not do away with nutrition or temperance, but it reframes and expands those elements and renders them far less central while also compatible with the whole.

In this section I build on my revised model and articulate some healthy, honoring practices of eating and drinking.[20] I lift up three elements that characterize eating practices that honor the body and build on a relational understanding of health. I deal with them in descending order of importance, even though they must be seen as integrated with one another.

1. *Eating is a sensuous activity that sparks enjoyment.* Just as our bodies are primordially created good, created for enjoyment and delight, so is the eating that sustains that goodness. Food appeals to our senses (tastes) in a way that is analogous to the way certain paintings, music, sculpture, and dance appeal to our sense of beauty. Like art, food engages us. Something is wrong if we fail to enjoy food.

We are sensuous, embodied, physical beings, and this characteristic permeates all our other activities whether or not we are conscious of its impact. Eating is so enjoyable, so much a part of God's intentions, that its underappreciation is almost a crime!

One reason I put this characteristic first is that taste is a wonderful mystery. Largely beyond voluntary control or even understanding, sensuousness is a gift of God. (Why does this pistachio nut taste great but that one taste woody? Why do I alone in my family like Tabasco?) Our bodily capacity for enjoyment is huge. Consider the first bite of a chocolate raspberry ice cream cone and how it generates pleasure. There is almost a quality of surprise to the delight we experience; that is, the tactile nature of food generates a strong positive emotional reaction. Where does that come from? What inner trigger does it set off? Our body has strange capacities that lie beyond, but also simultaneously, within.

The gratuitous nature of our sensuousness can put us in touch with God. Jesus' evident delight in eating and his gratitude to God sprung from his capacity for joy.

We too often stifle enjoyment and ignore sensuality. That is like turning one's back on a feast. It is a denial of life-changing gifts. It is almost a denial of God. In our practical section I will offer ways to increase our awareness/mindfulness of delighting in food.

2. *Eating ties us into the whole of the earth community.* By that I mean that the worlds of nature, both human and other, are involved in our eating. Paying attention to the quality of the food we eat makes us aware of the myriad factors from the nonhuman world that get on our plate. For example, a farmer friend of mine glories in his count of nightcrawlers per square foot of soil because their holes soak in moisture, aerate the land, promote great yields, and lead to the production of high-protein nutritious corn and eventually good bacon and ham. Most of these factors we cannot control, but we surely enjoy them for breakfast.

We also become aware of the chain of human labor that leads to our tables—from those who cultivate good seed (or not), practice ecologically responsible agriculture (or not), harvest, sell, and package food equitably (or not), and distribute its costs in a sustainable and just way (or not). We depend on those hundreds and thousands of people as well as those who manage the distribution and sale, foster greater nutrition, and pay attention to the impact of their decisions on rural communities. All this says little about the impact of slaughterhouse policies on the quality of animal life and the nutritional impacts of raising edible plants and animals in particular ways.[21]

Then there is the realm of those we eat with, those we relate to at the dinner table or the conference table. Eating with others is an act of intimacy or potential intimacy. Most of the great experiences I remember involved eating with friends or family as some part of the adventure. Eating alone, even a fine meal, is not much fun. Our physical and mental and social and spiritual health begin to come together on this horizon. In short, our health is part of the health of the whole. We can feel the sustenance of nutrition and of being borne up by others. We can be humbled by the gifts we have been given. We delight in the web that feeds us and that encourages us to share by feeding and nurturing others. I suppose at base this is why the church has considered eating a spiritual practice.

The importance of seeing our eating and drinking as connected to the wider conception of health is that we do not want to miss the "gift "quality of our lives. We don't want to miss the grace that infuses our lives and by which God reveals graciousness with every bite.

3. Eating involves balance between extravagant pleasure and scrupulous management. With this feature, for the first time, an aspect of eating that is within our volition comes into view. We have some ability to balance our appetite with our limits, and we may find in those limits a cause of joy.

This is where the virtue of temperance associated with the "scientific management" of our bodies and eating (or diet, that dread word) comes into view.[22] Indeed, we do have some capacity to say no to overconsumption in the name of honoring our bodily health, especially if health is conceived of holistically. This is because we have some moral goals—sensuality, relationality—that transcend our own narrow individual health. The revised understanding of health I am outlining will go far toward improving the health of those social groups—congregations, synagogues, other religious and Twelve Step programs—that can buy into the first two features of this account in some way. Furthermore, listening to one's body and eating slowly will naturally result in balanced, temperate—but enjoyable—eating. We do not need to overeat in order to enjoy.

Note that this reframing begins to address questions about the quantity and types of food we eat. There is a debate about which food pyramid specifies the optimal diet for us men and women. The food pyramid introduced by Harvard's Walter Willet[23] strikes me as more compatible with a holistic view of health than the conventional one. Willet's pyramid emphasizes at its base healthy exercise in sufficient quantity; this is certainly a broadening of the notion of what it takes to honor one's body.[24] The work of balancing what we eat becomes easier when we turn from viewing the work of abstaining from "bad food" (which we enjoy) to enjoying food in moderation.

If we see exercise as a necessary and fun way to honor our bodies, it is even easier. Finally, if we pay attention to the quality and source of the food we eat,[25] we will begin to eat well as we see our eating as a spiritual practice connected to the well-being of nature and distant peoples.

Learning How to Honor Your Body

Learning how to honor our bodies when it comes to eating involves at least three things: emotional and spiritual *attitudes*; *knowledge* about nutrition; and *habitual* experience. If we practice ways of honoring our bodies, we will be able to delight in living and share our gifts and abilities more joyfully.[26]

If the previous two sentences had been left unqualified, I would have bought into one of the most pernicious and most powerful myths in the world of eating: that individuals are in control of what they eat, and therefore that, if we are fat it is because we cannot control ourselves. This delusion is both pernicious and dangerous. This can be illustrated by the flyer I got in my newspaper this morning. Its heading read:

Macho
GRANDE
It's More than a Meal, It's a Challenge

What followed were the three latest offerings from a national Mexican café chain. The portions were gargantuan and, although a take-home box was offered, we all know that people eat more when they are offered more.[27] Furthermore, the appeal to masculine sexual appetite was apparent. If you fail to eat Macho Grande, then just how are you men defining yourselves?

It is apparent that the world of advertising and many other societal factors enter into our practices of honoring or dishonoring our bodies. (It's *not* just your fault!) Greg Critser's book *Fat Land: How*

Americans Became the Fattest People on Earth details many of the ways this happened:[28]

- food industry lobbying
- eating high-fat, high-sugar, processed foods
- our pace of life leads to fast-food convenience
- eating mindlessly or by oneself
- loss of funding for physical education classes
- vending machines in school or at work
- television-watching marathons
- cost of eating healthy food and cheapness of junk food
- a cheap food national policy and large portions of food
- sophisticated advertising of alcohol and other high-calorie foods (e.g., beef, doughnuts)

Consider what leads you to eat the way you do. How many of your habits can be traced back at least partially to social influences (for example, the number of calories in a restaurant serving or the ease of not exercising). From the previous list identify which social factors enter into your eating habits. It is a pernicious and dangerous myth that, in the face of these societal factors, individuals who are overweight feel as though they determine how they eat, that they are "out of control," that they are totally responsible.

Reflecting on What Body-Honoring Means to Us

1. What is your pattern of body-honoring? Can you eat almost anything you want and still feel good? Are you constantly dieting and barely holding the demon of weight gain under control? Do you enjoy exercising and find yourself looking forward to that? Do you like touching and being touched, or are you reluctant to touch and be touched?

Which of the following best represents your view of your body?

___ My body is a friend.
___ I am happy enough with my body.
___ Sometimes my body surprises me.
___ I really don't like my body.
___ My body betrays me; I can't control it.
___ I need to work on my body.
___ I can't remember a time when I was happy with my weight.
___ I love the feeling of working out.

2. There is a clear correlation between how we view our bodies and the way we eat. The following items are designed to help you find out what enters into the way you view your body. Rate them from 1 (no influence) to 5 (very influential):

    a. How I view my body has a great deal to do with my belief in God.

                1   2   3   4   5

    b. How others think about me determines how I honor my body.

                1   2   3   4   5

    c. I love to look good and to feel healthy.

                1   2   3   4   5

    d. I feel like I have a duty to take care of my body.

                1   2   3   4   5

    e. God cares about my body.

                1   2   3   4   5

    f. My own self-esteem leads me to honor my body.

            1   2   3   4   5

    g. Eating carefully is part of taking care of my self.

            1   2   3   4   5

I have discussed the emotional and spiritual factors related to honoring our bodies. Part of that we learned from our parents, our teachers, our marriage partners, and our kids. Whether we eat with the whole family at table, how often we grab convenience food, whether our spouse enjoys exercising with us—all these can influence how we eat and how we honor our bodies.

Is how we eat and how we honor our bodies central to our faith? Can we gather with other Christians (or simply other people) to covenant to work together on eating in healthy ways? That is certainly one of the dynamics behind the Weigh Down Diet, Jenny Craig, Overeaters Anonymous, Weight Watchers, and other groups. There is some bad news for Christians about the correlation between eating and religion in a study Greg Critser reports. In this study Kenneth F. Ferraro surveyed attitudes within religious groups and concluded that obesity was associated with higher levels of religiosity. The lowest average body weight was found among non-Christians and Jews while Southern Baptists and pietistic Protestants were at the top of the scale. Ferraro found an income correlation as well and opined that consolidation and comfort from religion *and* eating were available especially to the lowest-income people. Furthermore, religion did not appear to be operating as a constraint against gluttony and overweight. Ferraro bluntly concluded that pastors fail to bring up the subject for fear of "alienating the flock."[29] Many denominations are now attempting to remedy clergy's inattention to their own health.

When we turn from the church to our relationship with God, other questions arise: Does God care if we are overweight? Should we be striving after a perfectly slim body? Is this a cultural ideal or a spiritual one? What in relation to eating/honoring does God care about? What makes the way we eat a spiritual practice?

Information about Nutrition

An interesting switch took place recently. The conventional healthy eating pyramid that many of us grew up with got turned on its head and found a new foundation. Without going deeply into the reasons for this, it will be helpful to put the old and the new side-by-side so that you can note the differences. Most striking, perhaps, is the fact that the more recent pyramid includes exercise.

The opposite page shows the 1992 pyramid. The next two pages show the 2005 pyramid. (Note that the figure in the 2005 pyramid is exercising. It would be easy to miss that.) Then on the following page, Morgan Whitaker has translated the 2005 pyramid into one corresponding in format to the 1992 pyramid. Finally, in the last diagram I include Dr. Walter Willett's pyramid, which contrasts even more starkly with the 1992 pyramid. The more recent pyramids clearly stress the foundational value of exercise and the increasing emphasis on unprocessed and low-fat foods as the basis of a healthy diet.

1992 FOOD PYRAMID

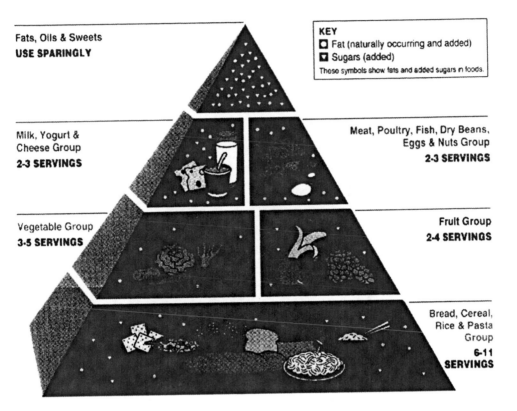

KEY
☐ Fat (naturally occurring and added)
▼ Sugars (added)
These symbols show fats and added sugars in foods.

Fats, Oils & Sweets
USE SPARINGLY

Milk, Yogurt &
Cheese Group
2-3 SERVINGS

Meat, Poultry, Fish, Dry Beans,
Eggs & Nuts Group
2-3 SERVINGS

Vegetable Group
3-5 SERVINGS

Fruit Group
2-4 SERVINGS

Bread, Cereal,
Rice & Pasta
Group
**6-11
SERVINGS**

1992 FOOD PYRAMID: United States Department of Agriculture, *Food Guide Pyramid: A Guide to Daily Food Choices,* prepared by the Department of Health and Human Resources (Washington, D.C., 1992).

2005 FOOD PYRAMID

MyPyramid
STEPS TO A HEALTHIER YOU
MyPyramid.gov

GRAINS   VEGETABLES   FRUITS   MILK   MEAT & BEANS

GRAINS Make half your grains whole	VEGETABLES Vary your veggies	FRUITS Focus on fruits	MILK Get your calcium-rich foods	MEAT & BEANS Go lean with protein
Eat at least 3 oz. of whole-grain cereals, breads, crackers, rice, or pasta every day 1 oz. is about 1 slice of bread, about 1 cup of breakfast cereal, or ½ cup of cooked rice, cereal, or pasta	Eat more dark-green veggies like broccoli, spinach, and other dark leafy greens Eat more orange vegetables like carrots and sweetpotatoes Eat more dry beans and peas like pinto beans, kidney beans, and lentils	Eat a variety of fruit Choose fresh, frozen, canned, or dried fruit Go easy on fruit juices	Go low-fat or fat-free when you choose milk, yogurt, and other milk products If you don't or can't consume milk, choose lactose-free products or other calcium sources such as fortified foods and beverages	Choose low-fat or lean meats and poultry Bake it, broil it, or grill it Vary your protein routine — choose more fish, beans, peas, nuts, and seeds

For a 2,000-calorie diet, you need the amounts below from each food group. To find the amounts that are right for you, go to MyPyramid.gov.

Eat 6 oz. every day	Eat 2½ cups every day	Eat 2 cups every day	Get 3 cups every day, for kids aged 2 to 8, it's 2	Eat 5½ oz. every day

Find your balance between food and physical activity

- Be sure to stay within your daily calorie needs.
- Be physically active for at least 30 minutes most days of the week.
- About 60 minutes a day of physical activity may be needed to prevent weight gain.
- For sustaining weight loss, at least 60 to 90 minutes a day of physical activity may be required.
- Children and teenagers should be physically active for 60 minutes every day, or most days.

Know the limits on fats, sugars, and salt (sodium)

- Make most of your fat sources from fish, nuts, and vegetable oils.
- Limit solid fats like butter, stick margarine, shortening and lard, as well as foods that contain these.
- Check the Nutrition Facts label to keep saturated fats, *trans* fats, and sodium low.
- Choose food and beverages low in added sugars. Added sugars contribute calories with few, if any, nutrients.

2005 FOOD PYRAMID: United States Department of Agriculture, *MyPyramid: Steps to a Healthier You*, prepared by the Center for Nutrition Policy and Promotion (Washington, D.C., 2005).

REVISED 2005 FOOD PYRAMID

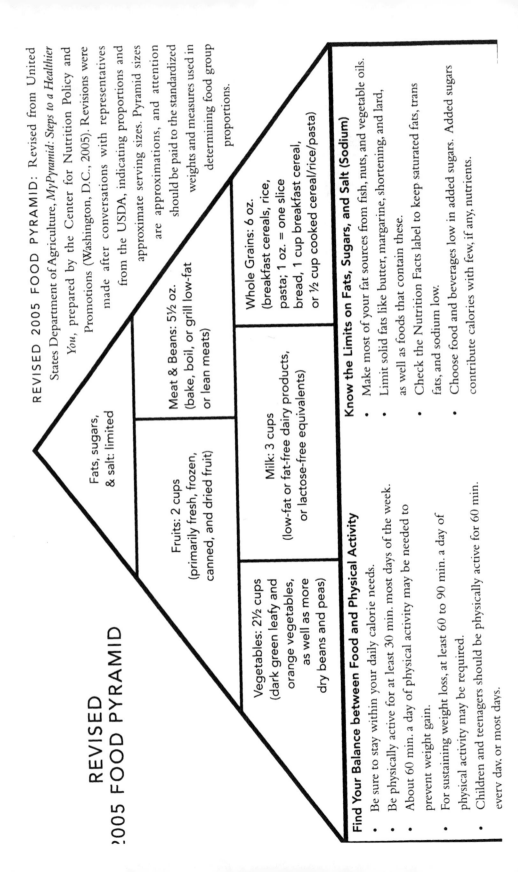

REVISED 2005 FOOD PYRAMID: Revised from United States Department of Agriculture, *MyPyramid: Steps to a Healthier You*, prepared by the Center for Nutrition Policy and Promotions (Washington, D.C., 2005). Revisions were made after conversations with representatives from the USDA, indicating proportions and approximate serving sizes. Pyramid sizes are approximations, and attention should be paid to the standardized weights and measures used in determining food group proportions.

Fats, sugars, & salt: limited

Vegetables: 2½ cups
(dark green leafy and orange vegetables, as well as more dry beans and peas)

Fruits: 2 cups
(primarily fresh, frozen, canned, and dried fruit)

Milk: 3 cups
(low-fat or fat-free dairy products, or lactose-free equivalents)

Meat & Beans: 5½ oz.
(bake, boil, or grill low-fat or lean meats)

Whole Grains: 6 oz.
(breakfast cereals, rice, pasta; 1 oz. = one slice bread, 1 cup breakfast cereal, or ½ cup cooked cereal/rice/pasta)

Find Your Balance between Food and Physical Activity

- Be sure to stay within your daily calorie needs.
- Be physically active for at least 30 min. most days of the week.
- About 60 min. a day of physical activity may be needed to prevent weight gain.
- For sustaining weight loss, at least 60 to 90 min. a day of physical activity may be required.
- Children and teenagers should be physically active for 60 min. every day, or most days.

Know the Limits on Fats, Sugars, and Salt (Sodium)

- Make most of your fat sources from fish, nuts, and vegetable oils.
- Limit solid fats like butter, margarine, shortening, and lard, as well as foods that contain these.
- Check the Nutrition Facts label to keep saturated fats, trans fats, and sodium low.
- Choose food and beverages low in added sugars. Added sugars contribute calories with few, if any, nutrients.

HEALTHY EATING PYRAMID

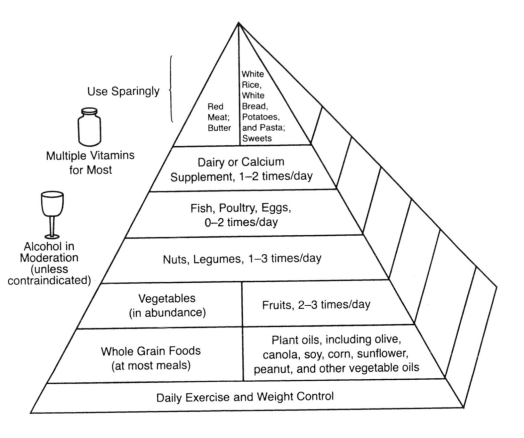

Use Sparingly

Multiple Vitamins
for Most

Alcohol in
Moderation
(unless
contraindicated)

White Rice, White Bread, Potatoes, and Pasta; Sweets

Red Meat; Butter

Dairy or Calcium
Supplement, 1–2 times/day

Fish, Poultry, Eggs,
0–2 times/day

Nuts, Legumes, 1–3 times/day

Vegetables
(in abundance)

Fruits, 2–3 times/day

Whole Grain Foods
(at most meals)

Plant oils, including olive,
canola, soy, corn, sunflower,
peanut, and other vegetable oils

Daily Exercise and Weight Control

Learning to Honor Our Bodies

1. Many people spend a great deal of time agonizing over their bodies but rarely come to terms with how they feel about themselves. For many people the concept of their body's acceptability is structured on the reaction of others and the huge number of cultural messages they receive about the "body beautiful." The result for younger people may be bulimia and anorexia. It is time to examine different views of ourselves. Initially this probably should be a private activity where you are asked to:

    a. Draw a picture of yourself as you see yourself.
    b. Draw a picture of yourself as others see you.
    c. Draw a picture of yourself as God see you.

    Usually this exercise deals with only A and B. The addition of C changes the whole perception. (Every person in a group setting should be given the option of "passing" on this activity, as it could be psychologically very difficult. Or they may wish to do the drawing but not be comfortable sharing.)

    A discussion may ensue about bringing the three visions into alignment. Should they be more similar? How does the addition of the person's feeling about his or her acceptability to God change the dynamic? The ultimate activity might be a prayer allowing group members to move toward self-acceptance.

2. Ask group members to bring in pictures of groups of peoples that are sharing an activity or life experience. What do their bodies tell us about the circumstances and philosophy of their eating? Examples might include photos of encampments from underdeveloped countries where starvation is occurring, pictures of an assembly of the religious, such as a church congregation or an assembly of Roman Catholic cardinals, pictures of young people at a rock concert or older people at a symphony concert. A final question: How does the body information in the pictures mesh with the life philosophy of the group?

3. Invite a nutritionist from a local health clinic or hospital to visit the group. This should be someone whose life work is in the field of nutrition. (Many internal medicine doctors who have patients who are obese or "morbidly obese," do not have the specialized knowledge needed to assist these patients.) Discuss the whole concept of dieting, including fad diets, the changing concept of weight loss, and the medical procedures open to persons who need much help. The floor under people who are sincere about weight loss is constantly changing. Every new study has a new view of "best practices." Discuss how prayer (including but not limited to grace at mealtime) may be an important factor in weight control and management.

4. Have each member bring to a group session a sampling of his or her favorite food (yes, you will have to choose). Let each, in turn, discuss the physical, psychological, and sensual properties of that food. Some questions that might be addressed are:
   - How do I feel when I eat this food?
   - Under what circumstances do I enjoy this food that contributes to it being special?
   - Why do more people not like this food? Why do so many people like this food?

   When participants introduce their food, they should do so in a celebratory fashion with a specially composed song, poem, or sales pitch. This needs to be done with passion and dedication!

5. What is food addiction? How does eating differ from other addictive behaviors? Should we treat food addiction as we do alcohol addiction or drug addiction? Stage a debate (not like the televised presidential debates, but like the formal debate format used in colleges and universities). This will require both sides to do intensive research on the nature of addiction. Invite a lawyer, speech teacher, or other person well versed in debate to listen to and comment on the persuasiveness of the arguments.

EIGHT

The Master Practice of the Lord's Supper

IN ANDREW, IOWA, there is a little Presbyterian church that has been there since the town was founded. That church has been the beneficiary of decades of service by students from the nearby University of Dubuque Theological Seminary and also from the John Knox Presbytery, which understands the value of small churches. I was honored to serve as moderator of the Session of that church for eight years. Basically this meant that once a quarter I went to Andrew, preached, celebrated the Lord's Supper, and moderated the Session (the governing body of local congregations) meeting.

During my first year or so, the church was so small that it seemed absurd to distribute the bread and wine by passing plates and trays among the six or seven people in the congregation. So we gathered around the Communion table and passed the bread and wine (actually grape juice) to each other. I would pass the bread and wine to, say, Sue Davidson, who was the elderly matriarch of the church. Sue would pass it on to one of the kids in the church who was always in danger of dropping the bread or spilling the wine. And so on around the circle. As each passed the elements, he or she would say, "The body of Christ, broken for you," or "The blood of Christ, shed for you."

Some Sundays it seemed a little disheartening to have so few in church. But whenever we celebrated Communion, it was clear to all of us that this was in fact "the body of Christ" and that we were the church of Jesus Christ in the town of Andrew and the world. I really like celebrating the Eucharist in a circle and, despite the fact that it got a little jammed in subsequent years as attendance grew, we continued to practice the Lord's Supper in that way.

Certain "master images" in the Christian faith guide both our reflection and emotional formation. We find ourselves influenced by those master images far beyond our conscious deliberations, using them also to reflect on our moral and spiritual decisions. It is almost as if the symbols are so powerful that they bypass our conscious reflection. I am impressed by the relative power of the involuntary and the visceral ways that we are formed and that our conscious reflections reinforce the visceral life.

One of those master images for Christians is the cross. Another master image, and the one that applies most directly to food, is that of the Lord's Supper or Eucharist. An image central to the faith, it is also a food practice that most Christians engage in four, twelve, or more times a year. Images, symbols, and practices (including rituals) reinforce each other and build up a potent visceral and reflective web of meaning.

Christians claim that the Lord's Supper is one practice of the church whereby we can get a glimpse of "your kingdom come, your will be done, on earth as in heaven." In Lutheran theology it conveys the body and blood of Christ and is a "foretaste of the feast to come." In Reformed liturgy it is a celebration of the "body of Christ, the bread of heaven." Indeed, in the Roman Catholic Mass it is understood as the very body and blood of our Lord. It is, at the very least, a ritual event that celebrates our memory of the Lord Jesus Christ. Thus the practice has generated high expectations, which only sometimes become actual experience. The image or symbol invites our reflection and invites us to actualize the significance of the celebration as far as possible.[1]

Discussion of the Eucharist, Lord's Supper, or Holy Communion can degenerate quickly into disagreement about the theological meaning of Christ's presence in the sacrament. I want to avoid that here. Instead, I want to identify and claim the *common* elements of the Feast that correlate with the features I described in the six practices investigated in chapters 2–7 above. What common elements of eating well are found in the Lord's Supper? What makes it a master practice for our everyday eating?

A master practice or model, by definition, excels in the qualities identified. It is the quintessential exemplar of the activity under discussion. In the case of the Lord's Supper, it is the best, the essence of what eating was intended to be, the very eatingness of eating.[2] Thus, our ideal practice of eating every day follows the pattern of the eating we do in Holy Communion, even though the quality of our eating can seldom if ever hope to match or realize the *ideals* contained there. If we catch a glimpse, get a foretaste, or realize the hope of achieving the ideal, it will not only be sufficient, it will be all joy.

Common Characteristics of Holy Communion

Contemporary liturgical theologian Hoyt Hickman believes that "whatever the Lord's Supper is, it is everything that eating is."[3] As we eat and drink, we have cause to evaluate what and how we feed ourselves, how we impact the environment, and how others eat. In short, the Lord's Supper is the master practice that guides all other practices, and especially those that have to do with eating and drinking. This is to put fairly heavy expectations on the actual practice of Communion and thus to encourage the celebrating congregation to practice carefully and deliberately.

The Eucharist itself is also a performative act in which we are in fact "performing" a way of acting. ("Performative" refers both to the dramatic quality of the practice and also to the fact that through our words we are "performing" a different world and living it.) We inhabit a somewhat different world during the ritual and say things that describe that world. Theorists of ritual understand Christian worship as an event during which communities are constituted, everyday life experiences are transformed, and our relation to the divine is expressed. Andrea Bieler testifies, "I believe the Eucharist has tremendous transformative power that can move us toward greater individual freedom and social justice."[4] The Eucharist is "holy eating," a master practice in which we gain some glimpse of the divine as well as the human ideal. As we are nourished, we learn to nourish others.

If Eucharist is a master practice, what are the elements that can shape our practice of eating? I identify five: (1) Eating is a joy-filled spiritual practice where Christ meets us. (2) Eating is a communion with God and others. (3) Eating can be formative, reviving our faith again and again in a way that is beyond our voluntary response. (4) Eating involves the material world and reminds us that we are part of nature. (5) Eating reminds us of our mission, the fact that we are interrelated with others in such a way that we wish to bring God's love to them.

Each of these elements is prominent in the sacrament of the Lord's Supper, and each enunciates or implies a feature of eating before God that guides the ideal way of eating and drinking. This is to say, the master practice of Eucharist guides our actions—not as a set of external obligations so much as a way of empowering us to act in ways that are appropriate to those who call themselves the "body of Christ." We are to act in ways that are appropriate to human beings in this earth community. The Eucharist is an exemplar of who we really are and what our eating and drinking really are at their (and our) best. I turn to the first of those elements now.

A Joy-filled Encounter with the Incarnate God

In chapters 2 and 4 I considered two practices that focused on joy and thanksgiving: saying grace and feasting. These are associated with the first characteristic mentioned above: recognizing Christ in the sacrament can fill us with gratitude and joy.

At the table of our Lord, Christians "meet" the Christ who gave himself so that we might live. At the table we can get a sense of the vast extent of God's love and self-giving for us. There we know that Christ reflected the unconditionality of God's giving, an unconditionality that is realized in creation as well. We see the goodness of God in our daily bread; we praise God for the delight that God embedded in all creation. We eat the abundance and tastiness of what God created for the delight of the creatures. (It seems important that the bread in fact be tasty and the wine or grape juice good.) We can experience a bit of the total goodness of God, who gives despite our unworthiness, who gives simply out of the joy of giving.

The response to such generosity is to enjoy and to delight in the good things of creation. We relish the food we eat, knowing that it is but one of the many things with which we have been gifted. Specifically do we celebrate at table the epitome of gifts: the life of Jesus Christ, which forms us into community and proclaims the total grace of our lives. We understand that God is accessible to us, that God indeed is watching over us even when we are oblivious to this.

As Christians we recognize that God in Christ is present at the table. This may range from those who affirm the sacrament as a memorial service to those who believe that Christ is substantially present. Edward Schillebeeckx articulates one Roman Catholic view when he writes, "In an earthly embodiment which we can see and touch, the heavenly Christ sacramentalizes both his continual intercession for us and his active gift of grace. Therefore the sacraments are the visible realization on earth of Christ's mystery of saving worship."[5] Gordon Lathrop gives a Lutheran perspective:

> Here, by the power of the Spirit and the words of promise, is the very *encounterable* self of Jesus Christ—his body—and the very *life* of Jesus poured out as the promised new covenant—his blood. All who are present who belong to that body are given to eat and drink, and food is sent to those who are absent. With Christ, then, there come to all the nations, to all outsiders, to us, all the riches and treasures, all the grace, all the judgment but also all the mercy of God.[6]

The Directory for Worship of the Presbyterian Church (USA) states that "Around the Table of the Lord, God's people are in communion with Christ and with all who belong to Christ."[7] Ruth Meyers, an Episcopalian theologian, speaks of Christian worship as "a saving encounter with Christ. We meet the living Christ, not merely the memory of one who lived, died, and rose nearly two thousand years ago."[8]

The most comprehensively agreed upon quoted statement about Eucharist is the document *Baptism, Eucharist and Ministry* (usually referred to as BEM).[9] The emphasis in that document points to the presence of Christ in Holy Communion, which is located not only in the elements of bread and wine but, even primarily, in the community gathered around the elements.

Joy and thanksgiving can characterize every meal. One practice that flows from this master practice is that we "say grace" before meals. Two characteristic aspects of "saying grace" are that we both adore and celebrate God's goodness, and we thank God for the bounty that God has provided us before we eat. John Koenig's name for the celebration, "the feast of the world's redemption,"[10] reminds us of a second practice that flows from the master practice, that of feasting in the Christian tradition. Feasts are times of great enjoyment that are usually scheduled for a particular season—Christmas, Easter, weddings, graduations, etc. They are times of special celebration at which we offer special *eucharista*—thanksgiving.

Community Building

In chapter 3 I discussed sharing and hospitality as basic Christian food practices, indeed as quite central to Christianity understood as a way of life. These practices are part of community building and living out God's purposes for food.

God's giving as Creator is universal in scope; everything that exists benefits from it. Giving back to God ideally then involves recognizing the common right of access to the goodness of creation by all creatures. God has, in short, created community. "The way God's giving is to be realized by us," writes Kathryn Tanner, "and not just God's intention, is communal or common. Individuals are to benefit only within a community in which all do so."[11]

Most liturgies recognize this communal feature; the Lord's Supper consists of sharing in the life, death, and resurrection of Jesus. It is an event that should empower community through people's reaffirming their commitment to be Christ's people. We eat and drink both in acknowledgment of common loyalty and in anticipation of being strengthened for discipleship. It is the community that Christ formed and, in spite of the fact that we are individually members of it, the community is nonetheless primary. Sometimes we get a sense of this community empowerment in our celebration; sometimes it seems as though it happens only in heaven. (Consider the graphic last two minutes of the movie *Places in the Heart*, in which those communing together include klansmen, black sharecroppers, murderers, murdered—those dead and alive, the alienated, and the beloved.)

When Christians celebrate the Supper, many churches will commission lay leaders or pastors to take the sacrament to others of the congregation who could not be physically present for the service. They acknowledge the wider community of members who are still part of the community though not able to be present. Similarly, the belief in the worldwide community of believers is recalled, both those who are celebrating here and now and those who belong to the communion of saints. We also talk of *communio*, the fact of the special relation of Communion that Christians share globally.[12]

June Christine Goudey maintains that the Eucharist is

rooted in human connectedness, a power-in-relation that arises from experiencing God in and through each other. . . . [I]t is the very act of eating and drinking together around a common table . . . that expresses this truth most profoundly. The Eucharist is "first of all an assembly . . . a community, a network of relations." We gather together as embodied, relational selves, and in so gathering we point beyond ourselves to the Creator who calls us forth.[13]

The assembly can be regarded as being called forth by God's yearning for us, God's very characteristic longing to be in relationship with us. God creates this community, this body of Christ, through God's Spirit-love and power. The Eucharist is one way God does this. When we eat this bread and drink this cup, we too are recreating the community. We are re-membering and reconstituting the community as the one that participates in Christ's life, death, and resurrection.[14] (This characteristic exhibits the two levels referred to in note 1 above—that is, although God creates this community objectively despite what we feel, our own sense or feeling of community is significant as well. When the Eucharist is celebrated rightly, the community God creates is more liable to be experienced.)

One way to live out the communal reality of Communion is to eat together after the sacrament. Such a communal gathering might offer the group a sense of public assembly and fellowship, of sharing. The efficacy of the early church's meals was the power of the Holy Spirit communicated through a set of social relationships formed and shared with each other at the table.[15] We can regain some of that quality in eating together after Communion as well as in the act of communing together. That power was essentially egalitarian as was Jesus' table fellowship, which brought healing to many and was a source of reconciliation. Indeed, many arguments and feuds have been reconciled at the Lord's Supper over the years. At the Lord's Table all are equally poor and equally rich.

When we step back from the Eucharist and ask in what ways its communal character might inspire our everyday practices of eating, one feature is clear: eating is a time for delighting not only in the food but also in each other. Eating together can heal old rifts, head off new ones, and build community. It is difficult not to find some means of reconciliation when one eats with others week after week. This seldom happens automatically, however. Eating together in community before God is a means of carrying on the fellowship and discipleship that Jesus initiates. Sharing one's meal with others is a time-tested way of building community in the church. It is a means of transformation for the people of God.

Community building goes beyond the church fellowship, however. The early church practiced agape feasts in order to welcome new believers. Christians today are under a similar mandate and have a similar desire to share their feasts with newcomers. Evangelistic outreach is often best practiced through eating events to which local residents are invited. Thus, welcoming outsiders to the fellowship is an important practice in the wider feature of community building.

In chapter 3 I considered ways in which our eating together builds community. There I explored the Christian practices of sharing and hospitality, aspects of our joyful mission to the world. Building community is itself a major Christian practice, a form of evangelism that is both outreach to neighbors and also continuous reconversion of ourselves who are believers. Fellowship and evangelism get infused into sharing and hospitality. Indeed, the way we practice sharing and hospitality are major forms of fellowship and evangelism.

Formative and Transformative

In chapter 6 I considered fasting as a practice that was particularly transformative. This feature is highlighted in the Eucharist as well.[16] Many have found themselves transformed at the Lord's Table.

When we come to the Table, we are invited to realize who we are. The liturgy of the Roman Catholic Mass has one of my favorite lines: "Lord, I am not worthy to receive you, but only say the word and I shall be healed." That is, we come, having been called to some self-awareness and confession and laying ourselves open to God's transformative power. We are reminded of our need to receive God's great gifts. The fact of eating bread and wine can make vivid to us our visceral need to depend on God and to rest in God's power and future. At the least we have this experience often enough to realize its power to transform.[17]

As we eat we are formed into being the body of Christ; our character and our self-understandings are reshaped. We are called into relationship with the community and also called to transform the world into the reality we experience at Eucharist. We are to glimpse, to experience, a vision of just what the kingdom is about, "on earth as it is in heaven."

The Table of the Lord calls us to be revived in our faith over and over again. We sometimes do experience the transformation of our motives and dispositions at the meal. There we begin to be formed into a community of faith, a community that needs to be reformed again and again, but also a community that forms others and addresses the world. The sacrament calls us to be what we confess we are, to be what we believe. It does something to us; better put, God does something to us through the sacrament. We are formed beyond ourselves, much as food continuously forms and transforms us through mysterious bodily processes. Our own initiative and openness to transformation are not inconsiderable. However, Communion does open us to our need for mercy and our capacity to participate in and to some extent at least reflect the life of our Lord. Not only our resolve but also our character and our reflection are changed.[18]

The Supper sends us forth with the mission to show God's love—the fifth characteristic we shall consider. Before we move there, however, we need to consider how the sacrament begins to impact our daily eating. There are certain preconditions that must be present if we are to be strengthened and disposed toward mission. What in-Spiriting practices might be engendered and reinforced from the formative and transformative nature of the sacramental performance? How do we get formed for mission? One way is through the practice of fasting (see chapter 6). Fasting is abstention rather than deprivation. It can be a way of being in solidarity with the hungry and, if practiced with others, even more powerful.[19]

Christians pray that they will increasingly live out God's presence in all that they do. They will be formed into the image of the one whose body and blood they celebrate. Earlier we considered that the practice of fasting might be a key contemporary spiritual practice. Especially today it is easy to get seduced by the culture of consumption in a way that is unmindful of what is entailed in our eating practices.

Fruit of the Vine and Work of Human Hands

The Eucharistic meal consists of food that has come from the physical soil, has been prepared by human hands (see chapter 5 above), and reminds us that we are physical as well. Thus we are called to honor our bodies to the glory of God (see chapter 7). We are to remember that the Eucharist is food.

The menu for the Supper is radically incarnational and also everyday, composed of simple, readily available, concrete, real things, the same real things that Jesus the Christ ate when he sojourned among us. The wheat and grapes that are key ingredients of the bread and wine connect us to the concrete, real earth. We are composed of the same materials and are connected in the same way that Jesus was to the ecological web. God the Creator made available the stuff of these central symbols and gives them to humankind to use, care for, and protect. These elements also make a statement about the incarnation of God into human protoplasm. The Lord's Supper should be celebrated with local bread and wine, the locally available staple foodstuffs that human beings live on.[20]

This connection to the earth reminds us that we too are made of earth, that we are only temporarily not dirt. Indeed, the environment flows through us as we breathe, drink, eat, defecate, urinate, and sweat. We transform the elements of bread and wine as well as orange juice and pasta into nourishment and blood, and that food becomes us. We grow food and it makes us, and we make love and war and politics and babies. Our own materiality/physicality is clear, and the sacrament of the Lord's Supper reinforces that reality.

The materiality of the sacrament ties us to the care of the earth and water by reminding us of our own erodibility. It calls us to care for our own bodies, which are part of the cosmos, integrally linked into all that is. Thus, two areas of Christian practice that the tangible stuff of bread and wine lead us to consider are the way we honor the earth and the way we honor our own bodies. Wendell Berry suggests that we cannot care for our bodies in any way different from the way we treat the earth. Surely, the obesity epidemic in Western nations, and particularly the United States (where 1 in 5 adults is more than 100 pounds overweight), suggests that we need to attend to the practice of honoring our bodies and the earth. This practice has a sense of urgency about it both because our ecosphere and our own bodies are being mistreated.

In chapter 7 I picked up this concern and considered how diet, exercise, and sexual activity are related to the qualities that Eucharist lifts up. How do we honor our bodies and live in harmony with our own nature and with creaturehood in general? We might well include a look at one particular foodstuff—alcohol—and how that is similar to our overeating in general. What is it that drives us to drink too much? How might the Eucharist address that?

Mission to the World

Holy Communion brings us face-to-face with God's love for us and for the world. In many ways the theme of mission to the world is interconnected with all the other elements we have identified.[21] What the Eucharist as an eating practice adds to the whole body of eating practices (which it encapsulates) is the aspect of mission. We who experience God's love in eating and drinking are to share that love quite physically and holistically. In imitation of Christ's gift to us, we "give to others with the hope that these gifts will be the basis for their activity as ministers of divine beneficence; one gives to them for their empowerment as givers in turn."[22]

Why the Eucharist in particular necessitates an engagement with the world that God loves has been made clear in *Baptism, Eucharist and Ministry*:

All kinds of injustice, racism, separation, and lack of freedom are radically challenged when we share in the body and blood of Christ. Through the Eucharist the all-renewing grace of God penetrates and restores human personality and dignity. The Eucharist involves the believer in the central event of the world's history. As participants in the Eucharist, therefore, we prove inconsistent if we are not actively participating in this ongoing restoration of the world's situation and the human condition.[23]

Karen Bloomquist, in a Lutheran World Federation document on *communio*, makes it clear that all Christians worldwide are coimplicated in the situation of any other Christian. This extends beyond our commitment to worldwide Christian brothers and sisters who share Holy Communion to all, because God loves us all.[24]

To participate in the supper means that we follow the example of Christ's healing the sick, feeding the hungry, and caring for all people. We become a sign of resurrection for many. Andrea Bieler believes that the third performative role that "holy eating rituals" plays often involves the "ambiguous process of death to life."[25] The act of eating and drinking itself involves the death of living creatures to preserve others. Moreover, acts of violence and destruction and starvation are rampant in the world. The Eucharist does not celebrate those; rather, it unmasks evil and sin. As a ritual of holy eating, "the Eucharist contains God's radical protest against this ongoing victimization and violence in our world."[26] Moreover, it also allows us to rededicate ourselves to the mission of loving others as God loves us.

The eating practice that is implied in the missional nature of Eucharist is our social ministry and care for addressing human need, especially the needs of the hungry and those who lack material sustenance. Perhaps it is the close connection of the Eucharist with human nourishment that has made ways of remediating world hunger such a pervasive concern of the Christian church. Many, if not the majority, of churches participate in food pantries, give to Heifer International, go on CROP walks, or give to their denomination's hunger fund. The practice of sharing food extends from those closest to us to those at great distances. Again and again we have emphasized hospitality and meeting the needs of strangers as central to the message and life of Jesus Christ.

In chapter 9 I consider the missional implications of the Eucharist, focusing on world hunger and practicing hospitality. The church is given the task of going out into all the world and lifting up the downtrodden, caring for the weak and poor. In this book we have looked especially at the issue of hunger because it is so clearly connected to the Lord's Supper. "The supper sends us away to be the body of Christ to our neighbor, to be for our neighbor what we have received in the supper."[27] Just as we have been nourished and forgiven, so we are called to nourish and forgive others.

Learning to Practice Eucharist

1. It is clear that, although Eucharist may be a model for Christian eating in that it incorporates many Christian eating practices, we may simply remain oblivious to this celebration. Why do you think this is true? Are there times when you are more appreciative of the Lord's Supper? What enables you to be more aware of the sacrament?

2. Could we celebrate the sacrament in ways that generate more of a sense of community? Could you imagine any ways of practicing the eating and drinking so as to feel more of a sense of fellowship and common participation in the Christian movement than now happens? (Can you imagine having a potluck after the service in which all the congregation ate together as a counterpoint to Eucharist?)

3. I wonder what children think about Communion. Do you
   know how your own children or those of others in church feel
   when Communion is being celebrated?

4. It seems important that we retain the sense of mission that the
   early disciples experienced in the Lord's Supper. Is there some
   way of incorporating more of the outward direction of ministry
   into the practice of this sacrament?

NINE

Living with *Jouissance*: Local and Global Action

WHAT, PRAY TELL, is *jouissance*? Let me tell you a story.

When my friend Malcolm was in college, the choir often went on tour many wonderful and varied places. Usually choir members were put up in congregation members' homes or with other hosts from the community. At one city, he and four other men were fortunate enough to get put up at what was almost a mansion. It was very plush, and everything had been done to ensure the comfort of the singers. Their group included four Lutheran Midwesterners and one recent immigrant from Yugoslavia (now Serbia).

In the morning the hostess asked the five what they wanted for breakfast. She said, "You can have anything you want—eggs any way you like them, ham, orange juice, bacon, pancakes, croissants, even steaks. I went out and got a lot of breakfast food for you so that you could have anything you like." The four Lutherans said that they didn't want to be any trouble and that they would like whatever was easiest and wouldn't put the hostess out. They would just like some cornflakes and coffee, if that wasn't too much bother—something that wouldn't be any trouble.

The hostess reiterated, "I would be happy to fix you anything you want."

"Oh no, no, that's okay. Cornflakes would be fine."

But Boris, the recent immigrant, the Yugoslavian, said, "Oh, that just sounds marvelous. I would like three eggs, over easy, and steak, and orange juice, and pancakes with lots of syrup."

The hostess began fixing breakfast. She really enjoyed cooking the eggs, steak, and pancakes. The four Lutherans ate their cornflakes in resignation while Boris was slurping down orange juice and cutting into a fine-looking steak. While they were looking at him, he poured syrup on his pancakes and, with the food threatening to run out of his mouth, told the hostess how great the breakfast was.

She was delighted. She had intended to make a real breakfast treat for these singers, and at least one of them had taken her up on it. The giving of the hostess was integral to her pleasure. Both the hostess and Boris experienced *jouissance*!

Too often we are like those Midwestern Lutherans. There is a feast laid out for us, and we cheat ourselves and God out of enjoying it. God (the hostess) has outdone herself and created a marvel, and we are blind to it. We just do not believe that God could love sharing like that. We settle for cornflakes when we could have steak!

That story reminds me of another parable. In the Gospel of Matthew (22:1–14), Jesus told about a king who was arranging a wedding feast for his son. When the sumptuous banquet had been prepared with ox and fatted calf on the menu, the king sent his servants out to those who had been invited. But the ones who had been invited turned their backs on the banquet and went their own ways. When the king heard about this, he sent his servants out to the highways and byways to invite any manner of people to the banquet, and they came and filled up the wedding hall.

The king in this parable reminds me of the hostess in the parable of the breakfast feast. They both remind me of the God who wishes for us the greatest *jouissance* there could possibly be.

The Path toward Jouissance

The message is this: Live joyously; don't cheat yourself! God intends that we take delight in and share food and eating. The way we eat may rob us of *jouissance*. It cheats others of our sharing, which can be our delight—and their survival.

Junk food, quickly prepared, thoughtlessly eaten, eaten alone or in front of the TV, and scarfed down—how can these practices not impact us? Is this abundant life? The ready accessibility and relative low cost of food—food made cheap through federal policy and corporate subsidies—leads to unappreciative eating, obesity, and poor health. It can also lead to attenuated relationships and to the transmission of misperceptions to our children. Rather than contributing to our delight and the enjoyment of our households, these dynamics have reduced the joy and quality of our lives.

We really want to eat well. We want to enjoy eating and to feel good about our bodies rather than eating mindlessly and unhealthily. In writing this book I aimed to work out—for myself and for you—how we can learn to eat well. The practices I have described here constitute a regime for eating healthily and happily. We can do this.

Jouissance is much more profound than just good feelings or even mindful eating, though it incorporates those. *Jouissance* is a matter of deep joy, of assured security, of living in the presence of God, as though the kingdom had come indeed. So this is not just a matter of enjoying our food, but a claim that *we can be transformed*. The eating practices the church has discovered and established over the generations are part and parcel of the path that will lead us to abundant life, to *abbondanza*.

These practices have a deep resonance with God's purposes and with our constitution as created beings. They are not separate or detached items on a list, nor are they discrete things to do independent of other spiritual practices or aspects of our faith life. They are integral to God's design for us. It is just that, for some of us at least, they are the most accessible and exuberant of God's ideas. They are a pathway toward other elements of the Christian life.[1]

Thus transformation starts with an acknowledgment of the deep invitation to the fullness of life that God has prepared for us.[2] If we do not understand that joy is the foundation, the substructure, of faith that undergirds our eating and our living, then our concern for eating degenerates into "strategies to use" during dieting or into fairly empty rituals. This can happen to our saying grace, for example. Our practices become disconnected from each other, rather than integral to the one goal of directing our lives toward God.

Without incorporating a sense of God's joy in us and God's yearning for us as a bottom line, even eating can become something we *have* to do to please God. With joy as a foundation, we learn to eat as a response to God's goodness, and we realize that this is the way things are supposed to be—the way we were created.

Toward the Joy of Eating

Here I want to become specific about what sorts of actions our eating practices might entail beyond themselves, that is, actions that can reinforce and further our eating practices. These further actions could be called "ancillary practices."[3] Ancillary practices are those that are improvised or devised for our time and situation, tied to historic spiritual practices, but especially appropriate for each group's particular situation. Thus there are master practices, such as baptism and Eucharist; historic practices, such as saying grace, sharing and hospitality, feasting, preparing food, fasting, and honoring the body (discussed in chapters 2–7 above); and ancillary practices, which express the values and meaning of the master and historic practices in ways that are especially suited to our contemporary situation and particular location. Different local churches could (and probably already have) easily devise their own ancillary practices. I will discuss some of these ancillary practices, but local churches are encouraged to discover or devise their own. Here I consider both the individual and the social aspects of ancillary practices. We can also think of delight and sharing as ways of organizing these actions.

Individual Delight

I turn first to individual delight. I have argued that our ability to delight is muted by a number of factors: overabundance, expectation of easy, cheap food, inability to share, concern to protect our privileged position, etc. The bottom-line reasoning that blocks our delight is mindlessness of one kind or another. While living the historic practices identified in chapters 2–8 will help to alleviate this, it is worthwhile to focus specifically on mindlessness and mindfulness as ways of supplementing and enriching these practices. This mind-set will enhance rather than compete with the practices.

In a popularization of her copious research on mindfulness, Ellen Langer first suggests several factors that account for mindlessness in eating and then turns to ways to deal with it.[4] In an era of triple-tasking, we form what she calls "premature cognitive commitments," fitting an activity into a predetermined mind-set and ignoring the present content of the activity. Much of Langer's advice about developing mindfulness comes down to putting process before outcome. Rather than focusing on the result of any activity ("getting finished eating"), being oriented to the process ("enjoying our food") can make us feel better about our lives and restore joy to them.

Developing a mindful appreciation involves reframing the activity of eating. It entails becoming alert to our food, table companions, and our own bodies. In the process of reframing, several steps may be helpful:[5]

1. *Preparing food.* Thinking about what one is going to prepare, finding a recipe, gathering ingredients, planning a schedule of cooking, setting the table, letting people know when the meal will be served.[6]
2. *Arriving at food.* Stopping to notice food, greeting others, and tuning into our bodies are all part of this. If we can be conscious of this, we will discover all sorts of sensations—smell, salivating, appearance, craving, others' reactions—at this initial point. Taking a moment to embrace this situation and accept eating this food will reduce stress and enhance the eating.
3. *Awakening to the food.* Saying grace for this specific food can awaken us to the sensations of the food, might help us consider its origin and preparation, and can open us to the wider

world of nature. We can become aware of the myriad forces that brought this food to our table.

4. *Tuning into our own bodies.* We can notice the movement of tongue, taste, fingers, lips, teeth, and stomach. How is our body reacting? We can be alert to how a candy bar versus a carrot affects our digestive system. We can be in touch with our need for food *and also know when to stop eating.* Food eaten mindfully will be easier to digest, and we will be less likely to overeat if we are alert to how full we are.

5. *Food cleanup.* We extend our awareness to include washing and putting away dishes. We work with others and in cooperation with them.

Other elements can also contribute to individual delight and enhance eating practices. Paying attention to what we eat, and not only to the process of eating mindfully, can be very helpful. Eating more healthily is clearly one way of increasing individual delight. This involves eating lower on the food chain. For example, the use of high fructose corn syrup in food processing has recently been discovered to trigger metabolic changes; in effect, it tricks us into eating more and storing more fat. This ubiquitously used substance does not stimulate insulin and leptin, two hormones that help turn down the appetite and control body weight. Nor does fructose suppress our body's production of ghrelin, a hormone that increases hunger and appetite.[7] We should avoid heavily processed foods in favor of raw or natural or organic ingredients.

Another element that can add to our individual delight is substituting a concern for the quality of the food we eat for the cost of food. This is difficult. However, good food is not much more expensive for middle-class people than highly processed, sugar- and fat-rich, nutritionally empty foods. The dividends that we realize in terms of feeling better will be adequate compensation if one can afford to shop this way. Gardening and growing some of your own food (even in an urban location) will also enhance your delight in eating. All people can participate in community gardens, and this might be especially helpful for those who find it hard to eat in a healthy way.

Fasting (chapter 6) and honoring one's body by exercising (chapter 7) are ways of delighting as well. The feeling of clarity we get by fasting and the high we get from exercising vigorously are delights in themselves. Time-pressed dieters (and who is not time-pressed these days?) can become more conscious of their bodily processes to enhance delight. One of these is that simply eating more protein at breakfast time (an egg or oatmeal or yogurt) will keep our blood sugar stabler and our appetite under control. Eating a high-protein salad and lean meat at lunch will prevent us from bingeing at supper. Feeling good about our bodies and their capabilities will enhance our individual delight.

Here are two of my favorite tips about eating. One is simply to fill up with vegetables or fruit or anything else that has high bulk and that persuades me that I have had enough to eat. Water will do this too. The other is that every once in a while I need to splurge, to enjoy a really great meal, so as to convince myself that I am not sentenced to any regime forever.

Individual Sharing

My second focus, on individual sharing, looks at the household or small group. At this level the sharing may take the form of teaching or consuming intelligently and in conformity with God's purposes and our bodily constitution. There is much that we can do as individuals to share our daily bread and to impact the well-being of other people and nature.

The choices that the family shopper makes at the grocery store, the farmers' market, the direct buying coop, and the subscription farm (known as a Community Supported Agriculture project or CSA) all play an important role in sharing. In this case the sharing has to do with how the person disposes of the household income; it is a form of stewardship. Shopping determines which people, groups, and businesses one will support; it is perhaps the most meaningful and effective form of political power these days. The individual shopper is the family representative and often both buys and prepares the food. Thus, she or he either is or is not sharing good eating practices and healthy food with the household or circle of friends. She or he is buying (sharing money) in ways that support local and environmentally friendly growing practices or supporting highly processed, nonseasonal foods that require high, wasteful transportation costs. To be sure, not all local foods are healthy and avoid wasting fossil fuels, but they stand a better chance of being and doing so. We consumers vote with our pocketbooks. Food from the farmers market or brought by the local grocery delivery is fresher and consumes less fossil fuel than others (consider West Oakland's Mobile Market, for example).[8] My sister-in-law buys her vegetables and fruit from a local Latino farmer who delivers them to her door. She writes out a list of produce that she wants that week and leaves it on the front stoop; he gathers up the items on her list and leaves a bill.

The preparation and care of food is another way that individuals share with others. Thinking about, gathering, researching (menus, diets, recipes), and preparing food for others is very real sharing. What sort of coffee, tea, or cocoa does the household use (see www. equalexchange.com)? How much time and attention goes into the preparation of a meal? Do we call each other to pay attention (be mindful) by the way we prepare food and present it to others in the household or in the circle of friends? We can invite the household to eat together some of the time and gather in a way that enhances careful preparation with attentive conversation around the table. Asking others to share a meal goes beyond simply ingesting consumables together; it is an opportunity to share our lives and public events. In this way we can begin and renew relationships and participate in one another's lives.

It is also a good way to make friends. Friendship is an essential ingredient in eating, as the old proverb has it: "Better is a dinner of vegetables where love is than a fatted ox and hatred with it" (Prov. 15:17). Gathering at a coffee shop or restaurant or home can be welcoming and can initiate and sustain friendship.[9] Also important to mention here is the area of advocacy. Men and women play important roles in advocating for a just and equitably distributed food system. Corporate bodies such as Bread for the World, denominational hunger programs, and Heifer International can sustain the efforts of individuals in doing this.

All of these ancillary practices of individual sharing supplement and fill out the spiritual practices of sharing and hospitality, fasting together, feasting cooperatively, honoring our own and others' bodies, and saying grace.

Most of the spiritual practices I explored in chapters 2–7 have both individual and social (corporate) components. It is also true that, after a while, it is difficult to separate delight and sharing.

Corporate Delight

The Christian faith assumes as a basic premise that the church is a community of equals. The table fellowship of Jesus, the communal nature of the early movement, the sacraments shared in common, and most of the eating practices all point to the community as the standard venue for thinking about the faith. This is in contrast to the individual base of the quasi-religions of success and consumption. It is therefore even more important that we recognize the way in which delight and sharing are corporate, communal practices. Among many such texts that articulate this conviction is Paul's injunction to the Corinthians: "If one member suffers, all suffer together . . . ; if one member is honored, all rejoice together" (1 Cor. 12:26).

In regard to ancillary practices of eating, instances of our delight in gathering are numerous. Eating is almost always involved in celebrations, in friends' getting together, and in festivities of many kinds. The Christian understanding of delight goes beyond this and maintains that any person's suffering and pain limits our delight. We are commanded to love the other as though we were that person, fellow Christian or not. The Samaritan did not ask the victim whether he shared the Samaritan's faith or whether he had anything at all in common with the other. Nor is there any indication that the Samaritan gains in any way from the interaction.

Delight and sharing go together, but I will artificially separate them for a bit here in order to highlight a number of ancillary practices that indicate how social interaction adds to delight. In *Simply in Season*, Mary Beth Lind and Cathleen Hockman-Wert counsel us—for the sake of our health, for the sake of taste, nutrition, variety, and the environment—to eat fruits, vegetables, and meats that are in season. They alert us to the way that sharing recipes (as they do) and shopping and gardening and working together add to the joy of eating. A part of their book focuses on the way that gradually learning to eat foods that are in season can be educational for families, for churches, and for other groups.[10] Many of those local foods are healthier than others. Many people join buyers' clubs to access these foods and to take advantage of lower costs.

One of the most enjoyable aspects of farmers markets is the social aspect. Such markets allow shoppers to visit with neighbors and friends, to get to know the farmers and producers, to meet and talk to strangers, and to be among people who appreciate many of the same things. Sharing our delight with others nourishes us; farmers markets bring the produce of the land and often handicrafts like pottery and dolls and sculptures and paintings into the town or city. Shopping on a human scale where you meet the grower and talk about where the corn and tomatoes came from and whether it is peak season or not, reminds us that we are corporately tied to the land as a species.

There are a number of options for buying food that bring delight. The u-pick farms (strawberries and raspberries, blackberries and apples), the farm stands, growing your own food in community gardens—all these are sources of delight. They are also ways to get to know your neighbors and to be in community with them. Portland, Oregon, has a wonderful community of eaters who publish a book entitled *Portland's Bounty: A Guide to Eating Locally and Seasonally in the Greater Portland Area.*[11] There are many such books and printed materials; for your area check the website www.foodroutes.org.[12]

Universities are also linking up their dining services with local growers to obtain fresher and locally grown produce. The experience at Yale was reported in *Atlantic Monthly* (October 2004). Yale has a course curriculum focused on growing foods; at one of the Yale colleges the house eats completely seasonally; there is also a project in which an overgrown lot was turned into an organic garden. Other universities have also linked the study of the economics and nutrition with their dining rooms. What a wonderful way to learn! Furthermore, these dining options are popular with students. Restaurants are linking up with local and organic growers who deliver healthier and tastier foods.

The line between corporate delight and corporate sharing is thin indeed. Graham Kerr, the "Galloping Gourmet" of PBS, makes this vivid in his autobiographical comment:

> My wife, Treena, and I chose to reduce our meat consumption by about $20 a week for our family of four adults. We spent ten of those dollars on vegetables we really liked. We lost weight, lowered cholesterol, felt better, and we enjoyed the change. Then we took the $10 savings, which becomes $520 for the year, and invested this new money into sponsoring children with an international aid agency. One child we still support today. He lives healthily in Ethiopia and has received a Christian education and wants to be a carpenter—all because of our habit change. How's that for a double benefit?[13]

One ancillary practice associated with fasting is to send the money saved by abstaining to a world-hunger agency. Other practices that are associated with corporate delight are feasting, saying grace, honoring our bodies, and sharing.

I would be remiss if I did not say that exercising together (playing racquetball rather than lifting weights by oneself) is far more enjoyable for me than individual efforts. I suspect that you can imagine many other corporate delights associated with food.

Corporate Sharing

Corporate sharing has three types of ancillary practices. First, those close to home will receive only brief notice. Second, there are wider ranging agencies and activities associated with sharing and hospitality domestically and internationally. Third, there is the whole area of political advocacy.

I have mentioned a number of cooperative arrangements for growing, buying, and even preparing food. Some organizations are more focused on sharing. One such is the parish-based community development, Work of Our Hands, an initiative of Roman Catholic parishes. Parishioners publicize the products and services they have to offer to each other. Directories publicize seasonal reminders of product availability; others exhibit at local community celebrations.[14]

Another is Community Supported Agriculture (CSA). These are farms to which households subscribe. Farmers deliver what is available to participating families who take the risk of poor yields but also the benefit of good yields. Some farms promote their members' manual involvement, and others promote educational visits for families.

A model combining many of these arrangements is that of the Food Circles Networking Project. This is a holistic system (or circle) that connects farmers, eaters, grocers, chefs, and processors. All maintain connections with each other throughout. The premier example of local practice is in Missouri (see www.foodcircles.missouri.edu/vision.htm). Its strategy is (1) to help farm families produce food for local markets; (2) to connect farmers and consumers directly together; (3) to strengthen those connections by encouraging community-based processing and distributing, and (4) to work with consumers and communities to encourage consumption of locally grown food.

There are also urban agricultural projects in which children are taught how to grow food. For example, there are urban community gardens in Milwaukee (www.growingpower.org) that form the backbone of a local and affordable food system in the inner city. There are Mobile Market and People's Grocery projects (West Oakland, California). There are congregations that support growing projects to feed local homeless shelters and also to give homeless people a chance to produce food and help others (Moorhead, Minnesota).

Thousands of Christians each week participate in Saint Stephen Food Banks, soup kitchens, food pantries, Saint Vincent de Paul, People in Need agencies, and other church-based agencies that share food with those who need it. Most of them probably say something like, "I always feel like I got more from being there than I gave."

Many churches are involved in offering hospitality to those who are food-insecure through shelters, Catholic Worker houses of hospitality, food pantries, and feeding programs. Some churches offer a meal on one evening a week to those who need it. Others offer breakfasts to school kids. Still others have emergency funds to assist in times of crisis. All these programs are sponsored by congregations, but often they are not publicized as well as they might be. If we saw them as ancillary spiritual practices by which the believers' own wholeness could be furthered by sharing food with others, then we might announce this discipleship opportunity more readily. We might see them as the valuable forms of ministry they are.

Let me turn now from those corporate practices of sharing food and offering hospitality[15] to those corporate agencies that depend on the participation of congregations and individuals to rectify suffering and need. I raise up traditional agencies such as Church World Service, the Presbyterian Hunger Fund, the United Methodist Committee on Relief, Catholic Charities, Lutheran World Relief, and a host of other church-based programs. I applaud as well the work of the United Nations International Children's Emergency Fund, the World Health Organization, the Red Cross, and all those other organizations that act in the name of their sponsors, either nonprofit or governmental or both, to relieve hunger.

Sometimes relief is the form of sharing that is needed. But in terms of long-term alleviation of hunger, there are other projects that are ingeniously devised. One of my favorites is the Foods Resource Bank (www.foodresourcebank.org). This organization helps coordinate the work of urban and rural congregations that cooperate to produce a crop. The urban church may contribute money—from youth group fund-raisers, women's organizations, men's work, internal mission dollars—toward the cost of inputs for a farm acreage. The rural congregation can contribute land and labor. When the crop is sold, the proceeds can be designated in three ways: toward the denomination's global development efforts, toward a particular development project to relieve hunger, or toward one of the development and hunger relief projects of the Foods Resource Bank itself (which works in some twenty countries).

There is much that a congregation or parish can do. One can serve as a frontline referral agency or clearing house and thereby direct hungry people to sources of aid, farmers and small-business persons to agencies that provide assistance, or parishioners toward local food outlets. Churches can help interpret for their members the practice of eating and explain what is happening to the nutritional content of their food when it travels long distance. They can support local farmers by opening their parking lots to farmers markets or their kitchens to direct sellers. Churches can invest in local community agencies. They can publicize sources of seasonal foods and local growers. They could include in the liturgy of their worship services an interpretation of spiritual eating practices and incorporate seasonal produce into their church decorations. Churches need to be concerned for the bodily health of their members, the health of the local environment, and the food security of all whom they can reach.

Another essential work requires an even more systemic and structural effort. One way churches have traditionally acted is through the advocacy of public policies. This can be done by writing to and visiting members of Congress, state legislators, municipal officials, and members of church governing bodies to encourage and support legislation that seeks justice, safety, and security related to food. We cannot assume that others will carry the responsibility for letting our opinions be known. This is especially true for an aspect of life that is so near and dear to our hearts and lungs and legs and stomachs and heads. This involves supporting legislation that expresses our values and beliefs and not merely critiquing legislation that does not.

One important policy to support if we want safe and nutritious food is to protect medium-sized farmers against the disadvantages that much recent farm legislation has implemented. The United States Department of Agriculture has a community-related division that supports farmers markets, Community Supported Agriculture programs, organic labeling, and beginning and minority farmers. Sometimes this legislation is not well supported, but the Campaign for Sustainable Agriculture, The Center for Rural Affairs, and the Practical Farmers of America (organic) are three organizations that lobby for these values. One ancillary practice is to enroll on the websites of these organizations and follow their lead in analyzing policy when we agree with the values expressed.

We can also encourage the work of such organizations as Bread for the World and our denominational offices that monitor the work of Congress, striving to keep their constituencies informed about significant decisions that are upcoming. Bread for the World is currently involved in a campaign to promote cutting hunger in half in five years and ending U.S. hunger in a decade.[16] Toward this goal it has succeeded in getting introduced into Congress the Hunger-Free Communities Act (www.bread.org). The National Catholic Rural Life Conference is very good about staying on top of legislation that would promote equitable and just conditions for food workers, farmers, rural communities, and the safety and nutrition of our food (www.ncrlc.org).

Another area that deserves our attention is that of fair trade policies that could benefit both U.S. and global farmers. Fair trade is essential to the safety, accessibility, and sustainability of our food sources. It is especially important to adopt policies that do not wipe out international partners (Mexican corn growers, for example) for the profitability of corporations that benefit from cheap corn and cheap food policies generally.

Workers' rights and safety are issues connected to agriculture. Beginning-farmer programs, which will raise up a new generation of farmers and allow the rural communities of this country to thrive commend themselves. The fact that poverty is disproportionately present in rural communities is connected to cheap food policies. An indicator of this is the fact that rural families depend disproportionately on food stamps. Rural people make up 22 percent of the nation's population but use 31 percent of the food stamps sold.[17]

Other policy areas could build up the social and economic capital of rural communities. These would benefit enormously from the support of the appropriate state and federal policies. Positively, there are encouraging signs of innovative energy industries springing up in rural America, especially wind and solar energy. There are also companies that can manage their business more economically and more efficiently from rural locations. Rural community development programs (which match those of urban programs) provide for fair access to markets and also provide the infrastructure that makes for fair livelihood, thereby contributing to our food supply.[18]

This brings us to the most important issue connected with food, that of ensuring adequate, nutritious food for all people. World hunger is a scandal in a world and for a country where there is enough for all.[19] We need policies that will enable all peoples to have access to a livelihood whereby they can provide for their children, their households, and their futures. It is a matter of grave concern to Christians if anyone does not have enough to eat. Clearly Jesus gave us the directive that we are to feed the hungry, clothe the naked, and visit those in prison. Equally clearly, the issues of health, environmental care, and economic policy all impact the issues of poverty and hunger. As Frances Moore Lappe famously said, the primary cause of hunger is poverty.

In their recent book *Ending Hunger Now*, former Senators Bob Dole and George McGovern along with Dr. Donald Messer make the case that world hunger can be eliminated.[20] They make several policy suggestions that churches can support in order to further the work of eliminating suffering around the world:

- Support school lunch programs domestically and internationally. This attracts the enrollment of many children globally and has the impact of cutting the birth rate as well.
- Support the work of the World Food Program and the UN Food and Agriculture Organization (FAO), both of them together called the UN Agencies on Food and Agriculture.
- Do all we can internationally to improve the role of women and the health and well-being of people who are in poverty. This will both cut the birth rate and enable people to support themselves.
- Support sanitation and clean water projects (Church World Service is big on this) and combat HIV-AIDS across the world.
- Promote programs that give poor people the technology and education that offers them the hope of a decent livelihood.[21]

Fortress Press has taken the commendable step of adding a website that provides further details on how to participate in organizations and projects that combat world hunger: www.endinghungernow.org.

Epilogue

THE RESPONSE OF NORTH AMERICANS to the natural disasters of Katrina, Rita, and the Christmas 2004 South Asian tsunami was incredibly generous. We have an enormously deep empathy for those who are overwhelmed by forces beyond their control. Many Christians are particularly sensitive to suffering and pain when they are caused by famine, drought, neglect, or epidemic.

Our sensitivity decreases rapidly when the disaster becomes routine. In the northwestern Sri Lankan town of Puttalan, just beyond the reach of the tsunami, Nicholas Kristof went to a shantytown composed of people who had been displaced by a civil war fifteen years earlier. There UNICEF workers showed him around a hospital "where a 13-year-old boy, Abdul Quadar, is so malnourished that he stands just 3 three 9 inches tall and weights just 26 pounds. The average 1-year-old American boy weighs that much."[1]

That is outrageous. But it has become routine.

World hunger is on the rise. Lester Brown reports that in the years since the Rome World Food Summit in 1966, when 185 world governments agreed to cut the number of hungry people in the world in half by 2015, hunger has actually increased. In 1990–1992 the number was 817 million people worldwide; that decreased to 780 in 1995–1997 but rose by 18 million to 798 by 1999–2000.[2] Bread for the World reports that by 2004 there were 842 million hungry people in the world![3]

And yet two-thirds of Americans are obese or overweight. Yes, this is a scandal of maldistribution. It is a scandal of poverty. But, even worse in my view, those of us who have too much don't enjoy eating. How can I possibly call that a worse scandal? That seems incredibly crass. However, I see the obscenity of world hunger and our own underappreciation of eating as linked phenomena. If we truly enjoyed eating more, we would want to share more. We would want to wipe out those conditions that produce a thirteen-year-old who weighs twenty-six pounds. (Thirty-five million U.S. citizens are hungry, up two million from last year.[4])

If Brown and other commentators on world food security are right, then there will be an increasing number of hungry people in the world.[5] Hunger, according to these reports, could well be on the rise. It will thus become ever more important in the future to share food with those who experience chronic hunger. Food security is threatened by many forces, including population increase, lack of water, rising global temperatures, war, chronic and persistent poverty, and plateauing crop yields.

It would be facile to claim that by participating in the seven practices presented in this book and thus enjoying food more we could wipe out world hunger. But I do think that it would contribute to our political and economic will to do so, and, for the most part, those are the missing ingredients.

God has been good to us. As middle-class and affluent North Americans, we have been spoiled with overabundance. We expect more. That is bad news, because more will not satisfy us; we will become bloated but not sated. Instead, God has given us Christ's eating practices as a way toward our own satisfaction. Sharing food points toward the community of God where all are full—the poor, the rich, and all those between.

Notes

Introduction

1. Michael Pollan, "The (Agri)cultural Contradictions of Obesity," *New York Times Magazine*, October 12, 2003, 43, 44, 46, 47. See also Pollan's, *The Omnivore's Dilemma: A Natural History of Four Meals* (New York: Penguin, 2006), 102-3.

2. Both this suggestion and the story of Anna's pumpkin were shared at the Lutheran Academy of the Rockies, Meeker Park, Colorado, June 22 and 27, 2005.

1. Practicing Eating

1. Leon R. Kass, *The Hungry Soul: Eating and the Perfecting of Our Nature* (Chicago: University of Chicago Press, 1994), xiii–xiv, 25–34.

2. La Leche League, *The Womanly Art of Breastfeeding*, 7th ed., rev. (New York: Plume, 2004).

3. Erik Erikson, *Childhood and Society* (New York: W. W. Norton, 1993).

4. Greg Critser, *Fat Land: How Americans Became the Fattest People in the World* (Boston: Houghton Mifflin, 2003), 132–34.

5. John Cobb Jr. *Is It Too Late? A Theology of Ecology* (Beverly Hills, Calif.: Bruce, 1994), and E. F. Schumacher, *Small Is Beautiful: Economics as If People Mattered* (New York: Norton, 1989).

6. See Michael Pollan, "The (Agri)Cultural Contradictions of Obesity," *New York Times Magazine*, October 12, 2003, 41–50.

7. See 1 Cor. 11:17–22 and Sara Covin Juengst, *Breaking Bread: The Spiritual Significance of Food* (Louisville: Westminster John Knox, 1992), especially chapter 4, on the meaning of Hebrew feasts.

8. See Caroline J. Simon, "Community, Rootedness, and Deliverance from Evil," *Perspectives: A Journal of Reformed Thought* 18:6 (June–July 2003): 12–18; Dorothy Bass, ed., "Shaping Communities," in *Practicing Our Faith* (New York: Jossey-Bass, 1997), and, on listening, resistance, and working for life-giving patterns, Craig Dykstra, *Growing in the Life of Faith* (Louisville: Geneva Press, 1999).

9. See Sallie McFague, *The Body of God: An Ecological Theology* (Minneapolis: Fortress Press, 1993), 51–53.

10. Stephanie Paulsell, *Honoring the Body* (San Francisco: Jossey-Bass, 2002), 11.

2. Saying Grace at the Labna

1. Cathy C. Campbell, *Stations of the Banquet: Faith Foundations for Food Justice* (Collegeville, Minn.: Liturgical Press, 2003), 238.

2. David Abram, *The Spell of the Sensuous: Perception and Language in a More-Than-Human World* (New York: Pantheon, 1996), 250–61.

3. Ibid., 260. Because they involve so many of our senses, eating and drinking may make our connection to the whole earth even more tangible than the air we breathe.

4. Deborah Kersten, *Feeding the Body, Nourishing the Soul* (Berkeley: Conari Press, 1977), 7.

5. See the article by Craig Lambert, "The Way We Eat Now," *Harvard Magazine*, May-June 2004, 50–58, 98–99.

6. While I obviously applaud this trend, it is important to note that attention to diet can take a managerial attitude by which we distance ourselves from our food. Instead, we need a spiritually holistic base that integrates our diet into our value system. Appreciation of ourselves as more than consumers is absolutely essential to that transformation in our value system.

7. Thomas Simons, *Blessings: A Reappraisal of Their Nature, Purpose, and Celebration* (Saratoga, Calif.: Resource Publications, 1981), 36–39.

8. Claus Westermann, *Blessing in the Bible and the Life of the Church*, trans. Keith Crim (Philadelphia: Fortress Press, 1978), 86.

9. Simons, *Blessings*. See discussion on 33–59, especially 33–38.

10. John Koenig, *Rediscovering New Testament Prayer: Boldness and Blessing in the Name of Jesus* (San Francisco: Harper Collins, 1992), 21.

11. Ibid., 49–50.

12. Ibid.

13. Monika Hellwig, *The Eucharist and the Hunger of the World*, rev. ed. (Franklin, Wisc.: Sheed & Ward, 1992), 6.

14. John Mogabgab, "Editor's Introduction," *Weavings* 7:6 (November–December 1992): 2.

15. Michael E. Williams, "Saying Grace: Living a Life of Gratitude," *Weavings* 7:6 (November–December 1992): 28–34.

16. Ibid. 33.

17. "Amazing Grace," *The Economist* 14 (March 1997): 31.

18. Sarah McElwain, ed., *Saying Grace: Blessings for the Family Table* (San Francisco: Chronicle Books, 2003), 110. This book includes table blessings from Hindu, Jewish, Islamic, Sufi, and nature religions.

19. See the interview with the founder, Carlo Petrini, in *The Ecologist* (April 2004): 50–53, or www.slowfood.com.

3. Sharing and Hospitality: The Basic Christian Practice?

1. Thomas Ogletree, *Hospitality to the Stranger: Dimensions of Moral Understanding* (Philadelphia: Fortress Press, 1985); Christine Pohl, *Making Room: Recovering Hospitality as a Christian Tradition* (Grand Rapids: Eerdmans, 1999).

2. *Time*, 163:23 (June 7, 2004): 57–113

3. Jeffrey Kluger, "Why We Eat: For Social Reasons," in ibid., 71.

4. Ibid.

5. Frances Moore Lappe and Anna Lappe suggest that food has become a link to who we are. "Embedded in family life and in cultural and religious ritual, food has always been our most direct, intimate tie to a nurturing earth as well as a primary means of bonding with each other. Food has helped us know where we are and who we are." "The Delicious Revolution," in *World Ark*, Spring 2002, an excerpt from *Hope's Edge: The Next Diet for a Small Planet* (New York: Putnam, 2002), 3.

6. See my "Autonomy as Justice: Spatiality as the Revelation of Otherness," *Journal of Religious Ethics* 14:1 (Spring 1986): 157–83, and "Spatiality, Relativism, and Authority," *The Journal of the American Academy of Religion* 50:2 (June 1982): 215–35.

7. David Abram, *The Spell of the Sensuous: Perception and Language in a More-Than-Human World* (New York: Pantheon, 1996).

8. Nearly half of all American families eat dinner together fewer than three times a week or not at all. See http://www.momcentral.com/necfamilydinners.htm or http://www.conagrafoods.com/media/news.jsp?ID=20030523.

9. Robert D. Putnam, *Bowling Alone: The Collapse and Revival of American Community* (New York: Simon & Schuster, 2000).

10. Richard J. Foster, *Celebration of Discipline: The Path to Spiritual Growth* (San Francisco: Harper & Row, 1979, 1998), chapter 8.

11. See Sallie McFague, *Life Abundant: Rethinking Theology and Economy for a Planet in Peril* (Minneapolis: Fortress Press, 2001), 55.

12. Christians claim that this characteristic of life was built into the world at creation, and that it does not require special revelation to recognize it.

13. Douglas John Hall, *The Steward: A Biblical Symbol Comes of Age*, rev. ed. with a foreword by Roland E. Vallet (Grand Rapids: Eerdmans; and New York: Friendship Press, 1990), 26.

14. Daniel L. Migliore, *Faith Seeking Understanding: An Introduction to Christian Theology* (Grand Rapids: Eerdmans, 1991), 85.

15. Monika Hellwig, *The Eucharist and the Hunger of the World*; rev. ed. (Franklin, Wisc.: Sheed & Ward, 1992). There is a balance here. One sometimes needs and likes to be alone, to think, to gather oneself, to be able to enter into a time of togetherness.

Aloneness may enhance even the quality of togetherness. I have exaggerated the value of sociability because I think it is threatened.

16. Ibid., 9. In some ways, this is the central claim of that book since it is linked to her christological beliefs.

17. Ibid., 12.

18. Henri Nouwen, *Reaching Out: The Three Movements of the Spiritual Life* (New York, Image Books, 1975), 66.

19. Pohl, *Making Room*, 5.

20. Ibid., 6.

21. For "A Sourcebook on Hospitality in Early Christianity," see Amy G. Oden, ed., *And You Welcomed Me: A Sourcebook* (Nashville: Abingdon, 2001). Her introductions to the readings should not be overlooked.

22. See Pohl, *Making Room*, 61–84.

23. Murphy Davis, Ed's partner at the Open Door, writes that "Without supper, without love, without table companionship, justice can become a program that we *do* to other people." *Hospitality* (the newsletter of the Open Door), January 1988, 8.

24. David Kirk, "Hospitality: Essence of Eastern Christian Lifestyle," *Diakonia* 16:2 (1981): 112, quoted by Pohl, *Making Room*, 34.

25. Pohl, *Making Room*, 119.

26. Jolene L. Roehikepartain, *Teaching Kids to Care and Share: 300+ Mission and Service Ideas for Children* (Nashville: Abingdon, 2000).

27. Ibid., 12–13.

4. Feasting in Community

1. June Christine Goudey, *The Feast of Our Lives: Re-imaging Communion* (Cleveland: Pilgrim Press, 2002), 172.

2. Richard Poppen, "Transforming Crisis into Opportunity," in Diana Stephen, ed., *Church and Society Magazine*, November–December 2004): 27–28.

3. See Pam Brubaker, *Globalization at What Cost?* (Cleveland: Pilgrim Press, 2001), for a demonstration of the way contemporary global economics enters Christian thinking.

4. Goudey, *The Feast of Our Lives*, 18.

5. Arthur C. Cochrane, *Eating and Drinking with Jesus: An Ethical and Biblical Inquiry* (Philadelphia: Westminster, 1974), 74.

6. Ibid., 40.

7. Ibid., 40–41.

8. On this point, see John Koenig, *The Feast of the World's Redemption: Eucharistic Origins and Christian Mission* (Harrisburg, Pa.: Trinity Press International, 2000), 93–95 and 82–85. "The emerging church in Jerusalem owed no small part of its missionary vigor to its liturgies of messianic feasting" (p. 85).

9. Ironically, most traditions that emphasize the Eucharist do not welcome everyone

to the feast. On this point there is a fascinating interchange in the *Anglican Theological Review* between James Farwell, who argues against the practice of open or inclusive communion (thus limiting communion to the baptized), and Kathryn Tanner, who argues in favor of open or inclusive communion. See in that journal, Farwell, "Baptism, Eucharist, and the Hospitality of Jesus: On the Practice of 'Open Communion,'" 86:2 (Spring 2004): 215–38, and Tanner, "In Praise of Open Communion: A Rejoinder to James Farwell," 86:3 (Summer 2004): 473–85.

10. Jonathan Edwards, "The Spiritual Blessings . . . ," in *Sermons and Discourses 1723–1729*, ed. Kenneth P. Minkema (New Haven: Yale University Press, 1997), 278–96.

11. Jonathan Edwards, "Pleasantness . . . ," in ibid., 97–115.

12. Ibid., 102.

13. Sara Covin Juengst, *Breaking Bread: The Spiritual Significance of Food* (Louisville: Westminster John Knox, 1992), 77.

14. Richard J. Foster, *Celebration of Discipline: The Path to Spiritual Growth* (San Francisco: Harper & Row, 1979, 1998), 192.

15. Ibid., 190. In light of that, what does it mean that authentic feasting has fallen into disrepair?

16. Ibid., 193.

17. Henri Nouwen, *Lifesigns: Intimacy, Fecundity, and Ecstasy in Christian Perspective* (Garden City, N.Y.: Doubleday, 1986), 98–99; quoted in Cathy C. Campbell, *Stations of the Banquet* (Collegeville, Minn.: Liturgical Press, 2003), 239. See also Isaiah 12:2–3; Psalm 16:11; 119:111–12; John 16:20–22.

18. Campbell, *Stations of the Banquet*, 240.

19. Patrick T. McCormick, *A Banqueter's Guide to the All-Night Soup Kitchen of the Kingdom of God* (Collegeville, Minn.: Liturgical Press, 2004), 28.

20. Walter Brueggemann, "The Truth of Abundance: Relearning *Dayneau*," in *The Covenanted Self: Explorations in Law and Covenant*, ed. Patrick D. Miller (Minneapolis: Fortress Press, 1999), 108.

21. See McCormick, *A Banqueter's Guide*, 17.

22. Veronica E. Grimm, *From Feasting to Fasting, The Evolution of a Sin: Attitudes to Food in Late Antiquity* (London and New York: Routledge, 1996), 192.

23. Alexander Schmemann, *Sacraments and Orthodoxy*, quoted in Harvey Cox, *The Feast of Fools: A Theological Essay on Festivity and Fantasy* (Cambridge, Mass.: Harvard University Press, 1969), 43.

24. Gordon Lathrop, "The Hungry Feast," a series of lectures delivered at Wartburg Theological Seminary 1977, on cassette.

25. See 1 Cor. 12:26; quoted by Campbell, *Stations of the Banquet*, 91.

26. Alexander Schmemann, *Celebration of Faith 2: The Church Year* (Crestwood, N.Y.: St. Vladimir's Seminary Press, 1994), 15.

27. Richard J. Foster and Kathryn A. Yanni, *Celebrating the Disciplines: A Journal Workbook to Accompany "Celebration of Discipline"* (San Francisco: Harper, 1992), 194.

28. For simple alternatives, see Milo Shannon-Thornberry, *The Alternate Celebrations Catalogue* (New York: Pilgrim Press, 1982), or another such catalog.

5. Preparing Food: The Forgotten Practice

1. My appreciation to Pamela Couture for helping me see that preparing food is a significant food practice.

2. Leon Kass, *The Hungry Soul: Eating and the Perfecting of Our Nature* (Chicago: University of Chicago Press, 1994), 195–225.

3. Jane Goodall, *Harvest for Hope: A Guide to Mindful Eating* (New York: Warner Books, 2005), 220. Michael Pollan, in *The Omnivore's Dilemma: A Natural History of Four Meals* (New York: Penguin, 2006) writes that "19 percent of American meals are eaten in the car," 110.

4. Goodall, *Harvest for Hope*, 221.

5. The recent debate about self-sacrifice in Christian theology lurks in the wings here. Performing menial tasks for others when they are not willing to reciprocate may hardly be glorified. There is a vast literature, but let me mention at least these two: Barbara Hilkert Andolsen, "Agape in Feminist Ethics," *Journal of Religious Ethics* 9:1 (Spring 1981), 69–83; and Valerie Saiving, "The Human Situation: A Feminine View," in Carol P. Christ and Judith Plaskow, eds. *Womanspirit Rising: A Feminist Reader in Religion* (San Francisco: Harper & Row, 1992), 25–42. Feminist theologians have made the point that if the norm of self-sacrifice or agape does not apply to both sexes, then it is but a sham.

6. Christine Pohl, *Making Room: Recovering Hospitality as a Christian Tradition* (Grand Rapids: Eerdmans, 1999), details many of these examples of hospitality.

7. Dorothy Bass, *Receiving the Day: Christian Practices for Opening the Gift of Time* (San Francisco: Jossey-Bass, 2000), looks at the way we spend our time and how spending time is itself a Christian practice. I commend this book to you.

8. *Sunday Missal, 2005–2006* (Ottawa, Canada: Novalis Press, 2005), 18.

9. See Richard J. Foster, *Celebration of Discipline: The Path to Spiritual Growth* (San Francisco: Harper & Row, 1979, 1998), chapter 8.

6. Fasting for Life

1. Quoted from Lisa A. Keister, *Wealth in America: Trends in Wealth Inequality* (Cambridge, U.K.: Cambridge University Press, 2000), 8, 9.

2. Of course, fasting and honoring one's body can ultimately be delightful practices as well.

3. Michael Pollan, "Our National Eating Disorder," *New York Times Magazine*, October 17, 2004, 74–77.

4. "The Second Hunger: Complicity and the Hunger of the Affluent," a paper I delivered at the Society of Christian Ethics meeting in Chicago, January 2004.

5. This is a complex phenomenon. In fact, some portion of these negations cannot be eliminated. However, from a middle-class perspective, this optimism may derive from the "just world" hypothesis—the idea that people get what they deserve; "they bring it on themselves." This is a quite comfortable position especially for those who

enjoy a temporary insulation from those negations. To the poor and those with lower incomes this often comes across as crass insensitivity.

6. See Douglas John Hall, "Courage to Change . . . the Church!" in a series of three lectures published in *Currents in Theology and Mission* 22:6 (December 1995), but also present in many of Hall's other published works.

7. Marjorie J. Thompson, *Soul Feast: An Invitation to the Christian Spiritual Life* (Louisville: Westminster John Knox, 1995), 84

8. Ibid., 86.

9. Ibid., 99.

10. John Calvin, *Institutes of the Christian Religion*, ed. John T. McNeill; trans. Ford Lewis Battles (Philadelphia: Westminster, 1960), 1242.

11. *The Journal of John Wesley*. Wesley refused to ordain anyone to the Methodist ministry who did not fast twice a week.

12. John S. Mogabgab, "Editor's Introduction," *Weavings* 19: 3 (September–October 2004): 2–3.

13. Ibid., 3.

14. Marilyn Chandler McEntyre, "Too Much with Us," *Weavings* 19:5 (September–October 2004): 40.

15. Mark Buchanan, "Go Fast and Live" *Christian Century* 118:7 (February 28, 2001): 17.

16. Ibid., 17.

17. Gunilla Norris, "Many Ways: Fasting towards Self Simplification," *Weavings* 19:5 (September–October 2004):10.

18. See ibid., 4–11.

19. For this statistic, see McEntyre, "Too Much with Us," 42. For a more comprehensive demonstration of the injustice of the global food supply system, see Shannon Jung, "Eating Intentionally," in *Justice in a Global Economy*, ed. Pam Brubaker, Rebecca Todd Peters, and Laura Stivers (Louisville: Westminster John Knox, 2006), 50–61.

20. We are here in the realm of moral psychology as well as of theology and practice. The empirical question, which I answer affirmatively, is this: Does a visceral acceptance of God's forgiveness enable us to love our neighbor? This is worth considerable investigation.

21. What insights about fasting come from Jesus' wilderness experience in Matt. 4:1–4? Consider especially verses 2 and 4. Why was Jesus fasting? What does it mean to "not live by bread alone, but by every word that comes from the mouth of God"?

7. Honoring the Body

1. It may be that this attitude extends to discipline in general. We may be losing the ability to discipline ourselves since so much comes so easily and conveniently to us. Because practices are disciplines, this is a serious threat. My theme throughout this book is that daily practices can teach us healthy and enjoyable disciplines.

2. Mireille Guilano, *French Women Don't Get Fat* (New York: Knopf, 2005).

3. Review by Julia Reed, *New York Times*, February 6, 2005, Book Review section, 12, 13.

4. See the article by Laura Fraser, "The Diet Trap," *The Family Therapy Networker* May–June 1997, which details a new movement that "argues that dieting causes obesity rather than cures it. Diets are doomed, it suggests, not because of shortcomings within the dieter, but because obesity—whether primarily genetic or iatrogenically created by dieting—is far more intractable than once believed" (p. 47). Another article in that same issue, by Mary Sykes Wylie, asks, "Has Food Become Our Mortal Enemy?" (pp. 23–33).

5. Michelle Lelwica, *Starving for Salvation: The Spiritual Dimensions of Eating Disorders among American Girls and Women* (New York: Oxford University Press, 1999).

6. W. B. Yeats claimed, "We only believe those thoughts which have been conceived not in the brain but in the whole body" (quoted by James B. Nelson, *Embodiment: An Approach to Sexuality and Christian Theology* [Minneapolis: Augsburg, 1978], 31). What if we have learned in church to think of bodies negatively? How does a belief that "the flesh" is in "bondage" relate to Yeats's claim? If our bodies feel like impediments, can we believe that their Creator is good?

7. Stephanie Paulsell, *Honoring the Body: Meditations On a Christian Practice* (San Francisco: Jossey-Bass, 2002), 79.

8. See the articles quoted in note 4 above.

9. Michael Pollan, "Our National Eating Disorder," *New York Times Magazine*, October 17, 2004, 74–77.

10. Ibid., 76.

11. Ibid.

12. See sections of Rebecca Todd Peters, *In Search of the Good Life: The Ethics of Globalization* (New York: Continuum, 2004), especially 58–65.

13. These products manifest the ambiguity we feel about our bodies. They are ways to control our health but, at the same time, they may mask more beneficial ways of realizing health.

14. Peters, *In Search of the Good Life*, 183. The next time you are on a plane, check out the in-flight catalog. It is loaded with gadgets that are way over the top.

15. Paulsell, *Honoring the Body*, 82.

16. See Michael Pollan, "The (Agri)Cultural Contradictions of Obesity," *New York Times Magazine*, October 12, 2003, 41–47. Pollan indicates how our consumption of fat and sugars produces heart disease.

17. David Abram, *The Spell of the Sensuous: Perception and Language in a More-Than-Human World* (New York: Pantheon, 1996), 260.

18. See Larry Rasmussen, *Earth Community, Earth Ethics* (Maryknoll, N.Y.: Orbis Books, 1996), 105. This case is being documented by the science of ecology; I acknowledge that, despite my negative comments about science earlier, only some scientific thinking is fragmenting and/or based on a goal of technological control.

19. Peters, *In Search of the Good Life*, 161.

20. Other aspects of honoring our bodies include our sexual lives, our exercise routine, bathing, dressing, etc. For these aspects, I again point to Paulsell's book.

21. See Eric Schlosser, *Fast Food Nation: The Dark Side of the All-American Meal* (Boston: Houghton Mifflin, 2001), for a description of slaughterhouses and the processing of our meat. See also Donald D. Stull and Michael J. Broadway; *Slaughterhouse Blues: The Meat and Poultry Industry in North America* (Belmont, Calif.: Thomson/Wadsworth, 2004).

22. Elizabeth Tefler, *Food for Thought: Philosophy and Food* (London and New York: Routledge, 1966), suggests that the primary virtue in regard to our eating is temperance. This is a part of virtuous eating, but I believe that gratitude is primary.

23. Craig Lambert, "The Way We Eat Now," *Harvard Magazine* (May–June 2004): 58.

24. See the contrast between the two pyramids as graphics on pages 121–22.

25. See Brian Halweil, *Eat Here: Reclaiming the Pleasures of Locally Grown Food* (New York: Norton, 2004).

26. I find it difficult to separate out aspects of body-honoring from other eating practices, or to reduce them to the "physical." These difficulties are instructive, because they point out how holistic a practice healthy eating is. You may want to access the Evangelical Lutheran Church in America's wholeness wheel at http://www.elca.org/health/wholenesswheel.html. That indicates the broadness of the category of health.

27. See, for example, Eric Critser, *Fat Land: How Americans Became the Fattest People in the World* (Boston: Houghton Mifflin, 2003), 38.

28. Ibid.

29. Ibid., 56, 57, quoting Kenneth F. Ferraro, "Firm Believers? Religion, Body Weight, and Well-being," *Review of Religious Research* 39 (March 1998), 224–44; the quotes are from pp. 236, 231.

8. The Master Practice of the Lord's Supper

1. Master practices have another distinguishing characteristic: they operate on at least two levels. One is the doctrinal history of the practice, which both articulates a set of beliefs and models the ideal experience of the practice. The other is the level on which I have been operating for the most part in this book, that of the actual experience of the practice. This double-level operation certainly applies to such significant practices as Baptism and the Lord's Supper. This may explain why this chapter appears to be moving between doctrine and practice. I try to stick to the second level but find it almost impossible and maybe undesirable to avoid the doctrinal altogether.

2. Another thing that makes it a master practice is that it contains elements and meanings of many other beliefs and practices.

3. Hoyt Hickman, as described by Beryl Ingram, "Eco-justice Liturgics," in *Theology for Earth Community: A Field Guide*, ed. Dieter T. Hessel (Maryknoll, N.Y.: Orbis, 1996), 257–58.

4. Andrea Bieler, "Christian Worship as Ritual: Eucharist as Holy Eating," www.psr .edu/page.cfm?1=62&id+570, Pacific School of Religion faculty article.

5. Edward Schillebeeckx, *Christ, the Sacrament of the Encounter with God* (New York: Sheed & Ward, 1963), 45.

6. Gordon Lathrop, *What Are the Essentials of Christian Worship?* (Minneapolis: Augsburg Fortress, 1994), 17 (his emphasis).

7. *Book of Order: The Constitution of the Presbyterian Church (U.S.A.)*, Office of the General Assembly, 2001, W-2.4006.

8. "Responses," quoted in Lathrop, *Essentials of Christian Worship*, 27.

9. *Baptism, Eucharist and Ministry*, Faith and Order Paper no. 111 (Geneva: World Council of Churches, 1982).

10. John Koenig, *The Feast of the World's Redemption: Eucharistic Origins and Christian Mission* (Harrisburg, Pa.: Trinity Press International, 2000).

11. Kathryn Tanner, *Economy of Grace* (Minneapolis: Fortress Press, 2005), 74.

12. John Calvin and other reformers were quite insistent that the word had to be preached in community and the sacraments interpreted as well as administered properly there. Those absent from the supper can be brought these holy things, but the meal has in effect been consecrated by the entire assembly. The Lord's Supper is a corporate act that takes place in assembly and that builds community in the assembly.

13. June Christine Goudey, *The Feast of Our Lives: Re-imaging Communion* (Cleveland: Pilgrim Press, 2002), 157. Her quote is from John D. Zizolulas, *Being as Communion: Studies in Personhood and the Church* (Crestwood, N.Y.: St. Vladimir's Seminary Press, 1985), 60.

14. See Lathrop, *Essentials of Christian Worship*, 29, and also Marjorie J. Thompson, *Soul Feast: An Invitation to the Christian Spiritual Life* (Louisville: Westminster John Knox, 1995), 11, where she states that "love is *God's hunger* for relationship with us. Has it ever occurred to us that God is starved for our companionship?"

15. See Goudey, *The Feast of Our Lives*, 71.

16. Susan M. Smith, my colleague in worship at Saint Paul School of Theology, suggested in a conversation that the transformative power of the ritual operates objectively whether or not we feel it. Also speaking to transformation is the power of the ritual to bond us to the transcendent purpose of a Center of Value. See Susan Smith, "The Scandal of Particularity Writ Small: Principles for Indigenizing Liturgy in the Local Context," *Anglican Theological Review* 88:3 (Summer 2006).

17. One thing that the central acts of worship, including the supper, do is to "welcome us to the full truth about ourselves: sorrow and hope, hunger and food, loneliness and community, sin and forgiveness, death and life. God in Christ comes amidst these things, full of mercy." See Lathrop, *Essentials of Christian Worship*, 10. Having "examined

ourselves" before God, we realize Christ's forgiveness. One thing that forms and transforms us, then, is our realization of who we are and the fact that we are confronted
with our own ambiguous nature, sin and forgiveness, the need for confession and for
transformation.

18. How it does this may be instructive. Andrea Bieler speaks of the Eucharist
creating a "counter-world": [T]he Eucharist opens up space for a counter-world and
interrupts our everyday life experience. Common oppressive structures of social behavior are suspended during the performance. . . . Through this ritual, we share a new kind
of solidarity and common experience with all members of the group as we leave our
daily reality for a short period." See Bieler, "Christian Worship as Ritual," 4.

We catch a glimpse of the way people are related in ultimate reality, and that
glimpse of the vision of who we are meant to be changes us. We see an egalitarian society where each creature has its own integrity in relation to the whole. We see *shalom*.
In leaving the table, we see how relationships are distorted and we are transformed by
that contrast. We are formed by the weekly or monthly celebration.

19. Sacramental generosity transforms the world into the "theatre of God's glory"
eternally. Being redeemed by Christ means having received the wisdom and the power
of God. John Calvin, *Institutes of the Christian Religion*, ed. John T. McNeill, trans Ford
Lewis Battles; Library of Christian Classics (Philadelphia: Westminster, 1960), 20:52.
Participation in eating and drinking every day reminds us of the grace and mercy of
God and can have a transformative impact on our lives. Do we live, eat, and drink to
the glory of God?

20. Many eco-theologians these days have retrieved the tradition of a sacramental
understanding of creation, which requires an element of materiality. After all, it is the
material, biophysical universe through which God is seen and known. Calvin in his
Institutes placed the Christian sacraments on the broader basis of nature, recognizing
that God can use one of God's created elements sacramentally. William Temple wrote
of a "sacramental universe," in which all of material existence is essentially holy, a
medium of revelation, and a means of grace. The creation is the sacramental expression
of the Creator. Similarly, Rosemary Radford Ruether finds in the Jewish wisdom tradition and in New Testament Christology that the whole cosmic community of nature
is alive, grounded in and embodying the divine Spirit who is its source of life and
renewal of life. John Calvin, *Institutes*, 4.14.18; William Temple, *Man, Nature, and God*
(London: Macmillan, 1934), 482–95; Rosemary Radford Ruether, *Gaia and God: An
Ecofeminist Theology of Earth-healing* (San Francisco: Harper, 1992), 229–37; quoted in
Brian McKinlay, "The Challenges to Sacramental Theology from Ecology Theology,"
http://members.tripod.com/~mckinlay/essays/e3142.html, 2–3.

21. Gordon Lathrop nicely encapsulates this connection in his reasons why the
essential things of worship—Word, Eucharist, Baptism—are central. These three "occur
at the heart of a participating community so that all people may freely encounter God's
mercy in Christ, that they may come to faith again and again, that they may be formed

into a community of faith, that they may be brought to the possibility of love for God's world." Notice the cumulative nature of the statement and how each aspect builds on the previous one (Lathrop, *Essentials of Christian Worship*, 22).

22. Tanner, *Economy of Grace*, 75.

23. "Eucharist," 20; see note 9 above.

24. Karen Bloomquist, "Engaging Economic Globalization as a Communion," Lutheran World Federation, May 2001, http://www.lutheranworld.org/What_We_Do/DTS/Globalization_EN.pdf, especially 19–20.

25. Bieler, "Christian Worship as Ritual," 5.

26. Ibid., 6.

27. Tanner, *Economy of Grace*, 18.

9. Living with Jouissance: Local and Global Action

1. I think rural members of the body of Christ know this especially well because they are close to the soil that is vital to growth and they know where food ultimately and mysteriously comes from. Rural parishes and congregations can develop and share this liturgical and life resource with other members of the body.

2. See Huston Smith, "Reasons for Joy: The Soul of Christianity," *Christian Century* 122:20 (October 4, 2005): 10, 11.

3. I picked up this term from Larry Rasmussen at the Lutheran Academy of the Rockies, July 2005. If the activity surrounding Anna's pumpkin in the story in the introduction (p. 4n5) were to continue, it might be seen as an ancillary practice.

4. Ellen J. Langer, *Mindfulness* (Cambridge, Mass.: Perseus Books, 1989).

5. See the blog "Mindful Eating," http://www.mindfuleating.org/MindfulEating .html, which was suggestive of this frame. It was interesting that the whole matter of preparing food was handled in the last step and then almost cursorily!

6. There are brackets around this item to indicate that usually not all those gathered will have participated in preparation.

7. See Janet Helm, *Chicago Tribune*, "Studies Point to High Fructose Corn Syrup as a Culprit in Obesity," reprinted in *Mobile Register*, October 18, 2005, 3D.

8. Gregory Dicum, "Produce to the People!" www.sfgate.com, March 9, 2005.

9. See, for example, Kathleen Parker, "Our Caffeine Communion," *Kansas City Star*, September 18, 2005.

10. Mary Beth Lind and Cathleen Hockman-Wert, *Simply in Season* (Scottsdale, Pa., and Waterloo, Ont.: Herald Press, Mennonite Central Committee, 2005).

11. Published by the Interfaith Network for Earth Concerns/Ecumenical Ministries of Oregon, 1999; e-mail inec@emoregon.org or call 503-244-8318.

12. For other websites see the appendix.

13. Lind and Hockman-Wert, foreword, *Simply in Season*, 2.

14. For a fuller description, see *Catholic Rural Life* (Spring 2004): 4–7.

15. See Christine Pohl, *Making Room: Recovering Hospitality as a Christian Tradition* (Grand Rapids: Eerdmans, 1999), for other examples.

16. Newsletter from Bread for the World, November 2005.

17. This is according to the Carsey Institute at the University of New Hampshire. In all, 4.6 million rural residents received food stamp benefits in 2001. See www.carseyinstitute.unh.edu/.

18. Two resources that address the policy dimension quite understandably are Presbyterian Church (USA), *We Are What We Eat* (approved by the General Assembly 2002; available by calling 1-800-524-2612); and the U.S. Conference of Catholic Bishops, *For I Was Hungry and You Gave Me Food* (2004, available by calling 1-800-235-8722). Both of these booklets build on a firm faith basis.

19. Craig L. Nessan, *Give Us This Day: A Lutheran Response to World Hunger* (Minneapolis: Fortress Press, 2003), compellingly and concisely makes the case that world hunger is a scandal

20. Bob Dole, George McGovern, and Donald E. Messer, *Ending Hunger Now* (Minneapolis: Fortress Press, 2005).

21. See also Leslie Scanlon, interviewer, "Former Senators Take On Needs of Hungry," *Presbyterian Outlook* 187:38 (November 14, 2005): 3–7, and Mark Douglas, review of *Ending Hunger Now*, in idem, 15, 19.

Epilogue

1. Nichols D. Kristof, "Waging a War We Could Be Proud Of," *New York Times*, January 10, 2006, op-ed page.

2. Lester R. Brown, *Outgrowing the Earth: The Food Security Challenge in an Age of Falling Water Tables and Rising Temperatures* (New York: Norton, 2004), 18.

3. Bread for the World, Hunger Report 2004 Executive Summary; see http://www.bread.org/learn/hunger-reports-2004-executive-summary.html. According to the report, the number of hungry people is rising at a rate of five million per year.

4. Ibid.

5. Brown, *Outgrowing the Earth*, makes this case. See also "Famine and Poverty in the 21st Century," www.ifpri.org/pubs/books/ufa/ufa_cho1.pdf; "The State of Food Insecurity in the World 2003," www.fao.org/docrep/006/j0083e/j0083e00.htm; and "The State of Food Insecurity in the United States," www.ers.usda.gov/publications/fanrr35/ (January 22, 2006).

Selected Bibliography

This bibliography focuses on eating practices and includes primarily entries that are more recent than 2002 and therefore were not included in the bibliography in Food for Life: The Spirituality and Ethics of Eating *(Fortress Press, 2004).*

1. Practicing Eating

Bass, Dorothy. "A Way of Life around the Table: Practicing Faith with Young People," *Clergy Journal* 81:5 (March 2005): 10–13.

Bass, Dorothy C., ed. *Practicing Our Faith* (San Francisco: Jossey–Bass, 1997).

Brenner, Athalya, and J. W. van Henten. "Food and Drink in the Bible: An Exciting New Theme," in *Unless Someone Guide Me* (Maastricht, Netherlands: Shaker Publishing, 2000).

Brubaker, Pamela K., Rebecca Todd Peters, Laura Stivers, eds. *Justice in a Global Economy: Strategies for Home, Community, and World* (Louisville, Ky.: Westminster John Knox, 2006).

Critser, Greg. *Fat Land: How Americans Became the Fattest People in the World* (Boston: Houghton Mifflin, 2003).

Dombrowski, Daniel A. "Eating and Spiritual Exercises: Food for Thought from Saint Ignatius and Nikos Kazantzakis," *Christianity and Literature* 32:4 (Summer 1983): 25–32.

English, Adam C. "Feeding Imagery in the Gospel of John: Uniting the Physical and the Spiritual," *Perspectives in Religious Studies* 28:3 (Fall 2001): 203–14.

Hellwig, Monika. *The Eucharist and the Hunger of the World* (Franklin, Wisc.: Sheed & Ward, 1992).

Jensen, Robin A. "Dining in Heaven: The Earliest Christian Visions of Paradise," *Bible Review* 14 (October 1998): 32–39, 48–49.

Jung, L. Shannon. *Food for Life: The Spirituality and Ethics of Eating* (Minneapolis: Fortress Press, 2004).

Kaza, Stephanie. "Western Buddhist Motivations for Vegetarianism," *Worldviews: Environment Culture Religion* 9:3 (2005): 385–411.

Pollan, Michael. *The Omnivore's Dilemma: A Natural History of Four Meals* (New York: Penguin, 2006). Contains portions of a number of articles quoted in this book and originally published in *The New York Times Magazine*.

Sack, Daniel. *Whitebread Protestants: Food and Religion in American Culture.* (New York: St. Martin's Press, 2000).

Saussy, Carroll. "Food, Glorious Food?" in *In Her Own Time: Women and Developmental Issues in Pastoral Care* (Minneapolis: Fortress Press, 2000).

Schlosser, Eric. *Fast Food Nation: The Dark Side of the All-American Meal* (Boston: Houghton Mifflin, 2001).

Scott, Peter Manley. "Anarchy in the UK? GM Crops, Political Authority, and the Rioting of God," *Ecotheology: Journal of Religion, Nature and the Environment* 11:1 (March 2006): 32–56.

Sutcliffe, Steven. "Children of the New Age: A History of Spiritual Practices," *Theology Today* 61:2 (July 2004): 274–76.

Thompson, Marjorie. *Soul Feast: An Invitation to the Christian Spiritual Life.* (Louisville, Ky.: Westminster John Knox, 2005).

Volf, Miroslav, and Dorothy Bass, eds. *Practicing Theology: Beliefs and Practices in Christian Life* (Grand Rapids, Mich.: Eerdmans, 2002).

Wallis, Jim. "Food and How We Get It." Special issue of *Sojourners Magazine* 35:5 (May 2006). Includes articles on the real cost of food, urban gardening, local food, and the Lord's Prayer.

Winner, Lauren F. "It's Called Junk Food for a Reason," review of *Whitebread Protestants*, by Daniel Sack, and *Fast Food Nation*, by Eric Schlosser. *Christianity Today* 45:7 (March 21, 2001).

Yocum, Glenn E., ed. "Religion and Food." Special issue of the *Journal of the American Academy of Religion* 63 (Fall 1995): 429–582.

2. Saying Grace at the Labna

Boulton, Matthew. "'We Pray by His Mouth': Karl Barth, Erving Goffman, and a Theology of Invocation," *Modern Theology* 17:1 (January 2001): 67–83.

Burkhart, John E. "Reshaping Table Blessings," *Interpretation* 48:1 (January 1994): 50–61.

Campbell, Cathy C. *Stations of the Banquet: Faith Foundations for Food Justice* (Collegeville, Minn.: Liturgical, 2003).

Cobb, K. "Table Blessings," *Christian Century* 103:8 (March 5, 1986): 241–42.

Emmons, Robert A. and Teresa T. Kneezel. "Giving Thanks: Spiritual and Religious Correlates of Gratitude," *Journal of Psychology and Christianity* 24:2 (Summer 2005): 140–48.

Juengst, Sara Covin. "'For What We Are About to Receive . . .'—Common Meals and the Lord's Supper," *Reformed Liturgy* 29:4 (1995): 242–46.

Kersten, Deborah. *Feeding the Body, Nourishing the Soul* (Berkeley: Conari, 1977).

Koenig, John. *Rediscovering New Testament Prayer: Boldness and Blessing in the Name of Jesus* (San Francisco: HarperSanFrancisco, 1992).

Marsh, Clive. "Did You Say 'Grace': Eating in Community in Babette's Feast," in *Explorations in Theology and Film: Movies and Meaning,* ed. Clive Marsh and Gaye Ortiz (Malden, Mass.: Blackwell, 1998).

McElwain, Sarah, ed. *Saying Grace: Blessings for the Family Table* (San Francisco: Chronicle Books, 2003).

Mogabgab, John. "Editor's Introduction," in "Saying Grace." Special edition of *Weavings* (November–December 1992): 2–3.

Simons, Thomas. *Blessings: A Reappraisal of Their Nature, Purpose, and Celebration* (Saratoga, Calif.: Resource Publications, 1981).

Thompson, Stephanie. "Fowl Pray: Tyson Gets Religion," *Advertising Age* 76:49 (December 5, 2005): 3, 84.

Yust, Karen-Marie, "Real Kids, Real Faith: Practices for Nurturing Children's Spiritual Lives," *Christian Century* 121:14 (July 13, 2004): 33–35.

3. Sharing and Hospitality: The Basic Christian Practice?

Boogaart, Thomas A. "Sovereignty and Hospitality," *Reformed Review* 57:2 (Winter 2003–2004). http://www.westernsem.edu/wtseminary/assets/Boogaart.pdf.

Foster, Richard J. *Celebration of Discipline: The Path to Spiritual Growth,* 3rd ed. (San Francisco: HarperSanFrancisco, 1998).

Heisey, M. J. "Circles of Caring: How to Make Mealtimes Sacred," *The Other Side* 25 (March–April 1989): 24–28.

Huetter, Reinhold. "Hospitality and Truth: The Disclosure of Practices in Worship and Doctrine," in *Practicing Theology: Beliefs and Practices in Christian Life,* ed. Miroslav Volf and Dorothy Bass (Grand Rapids, Mich.: Eerdmans, 2002).

Jung, L. Shannon, "Autonomy as Justice: Spatiality as the Revelation of Otherness," *Journal of Religious Ethics* 14:1 (Spring 1986): 157–83.

Lappe, Frances Moore, and Anna Lappe. *Hope's Edge: The Next Diet for a Small Planet* (New York: Putnam, 2002).

Lottes, John D. "Toward a Christian Theology of Hospitality to Other Religions on Campus," *Currents in Theology and Mission* 32:1 (February 2005): 26–38.

McCormick, Patrick T. "The Good Sojourner: Third World Tourism and the Call to Hospitality," *Journal of the Society of Christian Ethics* 24:1 (Spring–Summer 2004): 89–104.

McFague, Sallie. *Life Abundant: Rethinking Theology and Economy for a Planet in Peril* (Minneapolis: Fortress Press, 2001).

Nouwen, Henri. *Reaching Out: The Three Movements of the Spiritual Life* (New York: Image Books, 1975).

Oden, Amy G., ed. *And You Welcomed Me: A Sourcebook*. (Nashville: Abingdon, 2001).

Ogletree, Thomas. *Hospitality to the Stranger: Dimensions of Moral Understanding* (Philadelphia: Fortress Press, 1985).

Pohl, Christine. "A Community's Practice of Hospitality: The Interdependence of Practices and of Communities," in *Practicing Theology: Beliefs and Practices in Christian Life*, ed. Miroslav Volf and Dorothy Bass (Grand Rapids, Mich.: Eerdmans, 2002).

———. "Hospitality: Mysterious and Mundane," *Reformed Review* 57:2 (Winter 2003–2004). http://www.westernsem.edu/wtseminary/assets/Pohl.pdf

———. *Making Room: Recovering Hospitality as a Christian Tradition*. (Grand Rapids, Mich.: Eerdmans, 1999).

Poon, Wilson C. K. "Superabundant Table Fellowship in the Kingdom: The Feeding of the Five Thousand and the Meal Motif in Luke," *Expository Times* 114:7 (April 2003): 224–30.

Putnam, Robert D. *Bowling Alone: The Collapse and Revival of American Community* (New York: Simon & Schuster, 2000).

Roehikepartain, Jolene. *Teaching Kids to Care and Share: 300+ Mission and Service Ideas for Children* (Nashville: Abingdon, 2000).

Tanner, Kathryn. "Theological Reflection and Christian Practices," in *Practicing Theology: Beliefs and Practices in Christian Life*, ed. Miroslav Volf and Dorothy Bass (Grand Rapids, Mich.: Eerdmans, 2002).

Verhey, Allen. "Hospitality: Remembering Jesus," *Reformed Review* 57:2 (Winter 2002–2004). http://www.westernsem.edu/wtseminary/assets/Verhey.pdf.

4. Feasting in Community

Adams, Carol J. "Feasting on Life," *Ecotheology* 9 (July 2000): 38–48.

Brueggemann, Walter. "The Truth of Abundance: Relearning *Dayneau*," in *The Covenanted Self: Explorations in Law and Covenant*, ed. Patrick D. Miller (Minneapolis: Fortress Press, 1999).

Fagan, Brian M. *Fish on Friday: Feasting, Fasting, and the Discovery of the New World* (New York: Basic Books, 2006).

Foster, Richard J., and Kathryn A. Yanni. *Celebrating the Disciplines: A Journal Workbook to Accompany "Celebration of Discipline"* (San Francisco: HarperSanFrancisco, 1992).

Goudey, June Christine. *The Feast of Our Lives: Re-imaging Communion* (Cleveland: Pilgrim, 2002).

Grimm, Veronica E. *From Feasting to Fasting: The Evolution of a Sin: Attitudes to Food in Late Antiquity* (New York: Routledge, 1996).

Koenig, John. *The Feast of the World's Redemption: Eucharistic Origins and Christian Mission* (Harrisburg, Pa.: Trinity Press International, 2000).

Kuiken, Rebecca. "Hopeful Feasting: Eucharist and Eschatology," in *Hope for Your Future: Theological Voices from the Pastorate*, ed. William H. Lazareth (Grand Rapids, Mich.: Eerdmans, 2002).

McCormick, Patrick. *A Banqueter's Guide to the All-Night Soup Kitchen of the Kingdom of God* (Collegeville, Minn.: Liturgical, 2004).

Poppen, Richard. "Transforming Crisis into Opportunity," in Diana Stephen, general editor, "The Agricultural Revolution." Special issue of *Church and Society Magazine* (November–December 2004).

Schmemann, Alexander. *Celebration of Faith: The Church Year*, vol. 2 (Crestwood, N.Y.: St. Vladimir's Seminary Press, 1994).

Shannon-Thornberry, Milo, ed. *The Alternate Celebrations Catalogue* (New York: Pilgrim, 1982).

van Tongeren, Louis, Paulus G. J. Post, G. A. M. Rouwhorst, and A. Scheer, eds. *Christian Feast and Festival: The Dynamics of Western Liturgy and Culture* (Leuven, Belgium: Peeters, 2001).

Wright, David P. "Ritual in Narrative: The Dynamics of Feasting, Mourning, and Retaliation in the Ugaritic Tale of Aghat," *Catholic Biblical Quarterly* 64:3 (July 2002): 561–62.

5. Preparing Food: The Forgotten Practice

Andolsen, Barbara Hilkert. "Agape in Feminist Ethics," *Journal of Religious Ethics* 9:1 (Spring 1981): 69–83.

Bass, Dorothy. *Receiving the Day: Christian Practices for Opening the Gift of Time* (San Francisco: Jossey-Bass, 2000).

Dunn, James D. G. "Jesus, Table Fellowship, and Qumran," in *Jesus and the Dead Sea Scrolls*, ed. James C. Charlesworth et al. (New York: Doubleday, 1992).

Fiedler, Klaus, Paul Gundani, and Hilary B. P. Mijoga, eds. *Theology Cooked in an African Pot* (Zomba, Malawi: ATISCA, 2000).

Goodall, Jane. *Harvest for Hope: A Guide to Mindful Eating* (New York: Warner, 2005).

Grizzuti, Barabara. "PC on the Grill: The Frugal Gourmet: Lambasted and Skewered," *Harper's* 284 (June 1992): 42–50.

Johnson, Timothy. "Reverence for Life and Eating," in *Reverence for Life: The Ethics of Albert Schweitzer for the Twenty-First Century*, ed. Marvin Meyer and Kurt Bergel (Syracuse: Syracuse University Press, 2002).

Newman, Elizabeth. "Who's Home Cooking? Hospitality, Christian Identity, and Higher Education," *Perspectives in Religious Studies* 26:1 (Spring 1999): 7–16.

Saiving, Valorie. "The Human Situation: A Feminine View," in *Womanspirit Rising: A Feminist Reader in Religion*, ed. Carol P. Christ and Judith Plaskow (San Francisco: HarperSanFrancisco, 1992).

Stackhouse, Max L. "Godly Cooking: Theological Ethics and Technological Society," *First Things* 13 (May 19991): 22–29.

Tafoya, Maria. "Reverence for Life: Making Decisions," in *Reverence for Life: The Ethics of Albert Schweitzer for the Twenty-First Century*, ed. Marvin Meyer and Kurt Bergel (Syracuse: Syracuse University Press, 2002).

6. Fasting for Life

Adamson, Eve, and Linda Horning. *The Complete Idiot's Guide to Fasting.* (Indianapolis, Ind.: Alpha, 2002).

Berghuis, Kent. "A Biblical Perspective on Fasting," *Bibliotheca Sacra* 158:629 (January–March 2001): 86–103.

Buchanan, Mark. "Go Fast and Live: Hunger as Spiritual Discipline," *Christian Century* 118:7 (February 28, 2001): 16–20.

Duffy, Eamon. "To Fast Again," *First Things* 151 (March 2005): 4–6.

Frykholm, Amy Johnson. "Soul Food: Why Fasting Makes Sense," *Christian Century* 122:5 (March 8, 2005): 24–25, 27.

Hall, Douglas John. "Courage to Change . . . the Church!" *Currents in Theology and Mission* 22:6 (December 1995): 402–50. Much of Hall's work makes this or a related point.

Johnson, Jan. *Simplicity & Fasting.* Spiritual Disciplines Bible Studies (Downers Grove, Ill.: InterVarsity, 2003).

Jones, Gregory L. "A Thirst for God or Consumer Spirituality: Cultivating Disciplined Practices of Being Engaged by God," in *Spirituality and Social Embodiment,* ed. Gregory L. Jones and J. Buckley (Malden, Mass.: Blackwell, 1997).

Jung, L. Shannon. "Eating Intentionally," in *Justice in a Global Economy: Strategies for Home, Community, and World,* ed. Pamela K. Brubaker, Rebecca Todd Peters, and Laura Stivers (Louisville, Ky.: Westminster John Knox, 2006), 50–61.

Keister, Lisa A. *Wealth in America: Trends in Wealth Inequality* (Cambridge, U.K.: Cambridge University Press, 2000).

Lambert, David. "Fasting as a Penitential Rite: A Biblical Phenomenon?" *Harvard Theological Review* 96:4 (October 2003): 477–512.

Mogabgab, John. "Editor's Introduction," in "Fasting." Special issue of *Weavings* 19:3 (September–October 2004): 2, 3.

Ryan, Thomas. "Fasting: A Fresh Look," *America* (March 6, 2006): 8–12.

Searcy, Edwin. "Sustaining the Weary with a Word: Preaching Lenten Texts," *Journal for Preachers* 26:2 (Lent 2003): 3–8.

Towns, Elmer. *The Beginner's Guide to Fasting* (Ann Arbor, Mich.: Vine Books, 2001).

Webster, Robert Joseph, Jr. "The Value of Self-Denial: John Wesley's Multidimensional View of Fasting," *Toronto Journal of Theology* 19:1 (Spring 2003): 25–40.

7. Honoring the Body

Abrams, David. *The Spell of the Sensuous: Perception and Language in a More-Than-Human World* (New York: Pantheon, 1996).

Brown, Warren S. "Neurobiological Embodiment of Spirituality and Soul," in *From Cells to Souls, and Beyond: Changing Portraits of Human Nature,* ed. Malcolm Jeeves (Grand Rapids, Mich.: Eerdmans, 2004).

Butler, Lee H., Jr. "The Spirit Is Willing and the Flesh Is Too: Integrating Spirituality and Sexuality," *Currents in Theology and Mission* 30:1 (February 2003): 30–36.

Cox, Darrel, "The Physical Body in Spiritual Formation: What God Has Joined Together Let No One Put Asunder," *Journal of Psychology and Christianity* 21:3 (Fall 2002): 281–91.

Ferraro, Kenneth F. "Firm Believers? Religion, Body Weight, and Well-Being," *Review of Religious Research* 39 (March 1998): 224–44.

Fraser, Laura. "The Diet Trap," *The Family Therapy Networker* (May–June 1997): 45-52, 60.

Griffith, Colleen M. "Spirituality and the Body," in *Bodies of Worship: Explorations in Theory and Practice*, ed. Bruce T. Morrill (Collegeville, Minn.: Liturgical, 1999).

Griffith, R. Marie "The Promised Land of Weight Loss: Law and Gospel in Christian Dieting," *Christian Century* 114 (May 7, 1997): 448–54.

Guilano, Mireille. *French Women Don't Get Fat: The Secret of Eating for Pleasure* (New York: Knopf, 2005).

Hart, Alton, Lesley F. Tinker, and Deborah J. Bowen. "Religion and Nutritional Intake," *Nutrition Research Newsletter* 23:8 (August 2004): 16–18.

Lambert, Craig. "The Way We Eat Now," *Harvard Magazine* (May–June 2004): 50–58, 98, 99.

Leland, John. "Christian Diets: Fewer Loaves, Lots of Fishes," *New York Times*, April 28, 2005, G1, G2.

Lelwica, Michelle. *Starving for Salvation: The Spiritual Dimensions of Eating Disorders among American Girls and Women* (New York: Oxford University Press, 1999.)

McMinn, Mark R., and Stephen B. James. "Traditional and Biobehavioral Information in Dieting: Anticipated Effects of Christian Weight Loss Literature," *Journal of Psychology and Theology* 15:2 (Summer 1987): 132–40.

Nelson, James. *Embodiment: An Approach to Sexuality and Christian Theology* (Minneapolis: Augsburg Fortress, 1978).

Owens, Virginia Stem. "The Fatted Faithful: Why the Church May Be Harmful to Your Waistline," *Christianity Today* 43 (January 11, 1999): 70–73.

Paulsell, Stephanie. "Body Language: Clothing Ourselves and Others," *Christian Century* 119:2 (January 16–23, 2002): 18–24.

———. *Honoring the Body: Meditations on a Christian Practice.* (San Francisco: Jossey-Bass, 2002).

Peters, Rebecca Todd. *In Search of the Good Life: The Ethics of Globalization* (New York: Continuum, 2004).

Rasmussen, Larry. *Earth Community, Earth Ethics* (Maryknoll, N.Y.: Orbis, 1996).

Resnicow, Ken, et al. "Body and Soul: A Dietary Intervention Conducted through African-American Churches," *American Journal of Preventive Medicine* 27:2 (August 2004): 97–105.

Rouse, Carolyn, and Janet Hoskins. "Purity, Soul Food, and Sunni Islam: Explorations at the Intersection of Consumption and Resistance," *Cultural Anthropology* 19:2 (May 2004): 226–49.

Shogren, Gary Steven. "Is the Kingdom of God about Eating and Drinking or Isn't It? (Romans 14:17)," *Novum Testamentum* 42:3 (2000): 238–56.

Takahashi, Melanie, and Tim Olaveson. "Music, Dancing, and Raving Bodies: Raving as Spirituality in the Central Canadian Rave Scene," *Journal of Ritual Studies* 17:2 (2003): 72–96.

Tefler, Elizabeth. *Food for Thought: Philosophy and Food* (New York: Routledge, 1996).

8. The Master Practice of the Lord's Supper

Ayieko, Miriam K. "The Eucharistic Meal for Christian Life," *African Ecclesial Review* 42:5–6 (October–December 2000): 212–16.

Bangert, Mark. "Holy Communion: Taste and See," in *Inside Out: Worship in an Age of Mission*, ed. Thomas Schattauer (Minneapolis: Fortress Press, 1999).

Baptism, Eucharist and Ministry, Faith and Order Paper no. 111 (Geneva: World Council of Churches, 1982).

Baumgarten, Albert I. "Finding Oneself in a Sectarian Context: A Sectarian's Food and Its Implications," in *Self, Soul and Body in Religious Experience*, ed. A. I. Baumgarten, J. Assmann, and G. G. Stroumsa (Boston: Brill, 1998).

Bieler, Andrea. "Christian Worship as Ritual: Eucharist as Holy Eating," in Pacific School of Religion Faculty Articles and Sermons, www.psr.edu/page.cfm?1=62&id+570 (2004).

Bloomquist, Karen. "Engaging Economic Globalization as a Communion," Lutheran World Federation, May 2001, http://www.lutheranworld.org/What_We_Do/DTS/Globalization_EN.pdf; "Engaging Economic Globalization as Church," *The Ecumenical Review* 53:4 (October 2001): 493–500.

Boureux, Christophe, Janet Martin Soskice, and Luiz Carlos Susin, eds. *Hunger, Bread and Eucharist*, Concilium (London: SCM, 2005).

Gibson, Paul. "Eucharistic Food—May We Substitute?" *Worship* 76:5 (September 2002): 445–55.

Hickman, Hoyt. "Eco-justice Liturgics," in *Theology for Earth Community: A Field Guide*, ed. Dieter Hessel (Maryknoll, N.Y.: Orbis, 1996).

Hunsinger, George. "The Bread That We Break: Towards a Chalcedonian Resolution of the Eucharistic Controversies," *Princeton Seminary Bulletin* 24:2 (2003): 241–58.

Joncas, Michael. "Tasting the Kingdom of God: The Meal Ministry of Jesus and Its Implications for Contemporary Worship and Life," *Worship* 74:4 (July 2000): 329–65.

Lathrop, Gordon. *What Are the Essentials of Christian Worship?* (Minneapolis: Augsburg Fortress, 1994).

May, George. "The Lord's Supper: Ritual of Relationship? Making a Meal of It in Corinth, Part 2: Meals at Corinth," *Reformed Theological Review* 61:1 (April 2002): 1–18.

McCormick, Patrick T. "How Could We Break the Lord's Bread in a Foreign Land? The Eucharist in 'Diet America'," *Horizons* 25 (Spring 1998): 43–57.

Mitchell, Nathan. "Communion: The Power of Emptiness," *Worship* 78:6 (November 2004): 540–50.

Ostdiek, Gilbert. "Who's Invited," *Word & World* 17 (Winter 1997): 67–72.

Purcell, Michael. "An Agape of Eating: The Eucharist as Substitution (Levinas)," *Bijdragen* 57:3 (1996): 318–36.

Routledge, Robin L. "Passover and Last Supper," *Tyndale Bulletin* 53:2 (2002): 203–21.

Rubin, Miri. "Whose Eucharist? Eucharistic Identity as Historical Subject," *Modern Theology* 15 (April 1999): 197–208.

Sack, Daniel. "Every Meal Has a Meaning: Church Suppers Feed the Body and the Soul," *Christian Ministry* 30 (May–June 1999): 14–17.

Smith, Susan. "The Scandal of Particularity Writ Small: Principles for Indigenizing Liturgy in the Local Context," *Anglican Theological Review* 88:3 (Summer 2006).

Strohl, Jane E. "God's Self-Revelation in the Sacrament of the Altar," in *By Faith Alone: Essays on Justification in Honor of Gerald O. Forde*, ed. Joseph A. Burgess and Marc Kolden (Grand Rapids, Mich.: Eerdmans, 2004).

Tanner, Kathryn. *Economy of Grace* (Minneapolis: Fortress Press, 2005).

Thomas, Philip H. E. "Anglicans and Communion: Six Propositions and an Invitation to Participate in the Communion Study," *Anglican Theological Review* 85:3 (Summer 2003): 511–21.

Weatherly, Jon A. "Eating and Drinking in the Kingdom of God: The Emmaus Episode and the Meal Motif in Luke-Acts," in *Christ's Victorious Church: Essays on Biblical Ecclesiology and Eschatology in Honor of Tom Friskney* (Eugene, Oregon: Wipf and Stock, 2001).

Welker, Michael. "Holy Spirit and Holy Communion," *Word & World* 23:2 (Spring 2003): 154–59.

Zirkel, Patricia McCormick. "The Body of Christ and the Future of Liturgy," *Anglican Theological Review* 81:3 (Summer 1999): 451–68.

Zizioulas, John D. *Being as Communion: Studies in Personhood and the Church* (Crestwood, N.Y.: St. Vladimir's Seminary Press, 1985).

9. Living with Jouissance: Local and Global Action

Danker, William J., and Paul R. Malte, eds. *Hungry Need Not Die—Unless We Think So* (St. Louis, Mo.: Board of Social Ministry and World Relief, Lutheran Church-Missouri Synod, 1977).

Desjardins, Michel. "Teaching about Religion with Food," *Teaching Theology and Religion* 7:3 (July 2004): 153–58.

Dole, Bob, George McGovern, and Donald E. Messer. *Ending Hunger Now: A Challenge to Persons of Faith* (Minneapolis: Fortress Press, 2005).

U.S. Conference of Catholic Bishops. *For I Was Hungry and You Gave Me Food* (Washington, D.C., 2004). To obtain this resource, call 800-235-8722.

Halweil, Brian. *Eat Here: Reclaiming the Pleasures of Locally Grown Food* (New York: Norton, 2004).

Helm, Janet. "A Sticky Debate: Studies Point to High Fructose Corn Syrup as a Culprit in Obesity," *Chicago Tribune*, 21 September 2005, Good Eating Section, 3.

Henderson, Suzanne Watts. "'If Anyone Hungers . . .': An Integrated Reading of 1 Cor. 11:17–34," *New Testament Studies* 48:2 (April 2002): 195–208.

Langer, Ellen J. *Mindfulness* (Reading, Mass: Addison-Wesley, 1990).

Lind, Mary Beth, and Cathleen Hockman-Wert. *Simply in Season: A World Community Cookbook* (Scottsdale, Pa.: Herald, 2005).

Nessan, Craig. *Give Us This Day: A Lutheran Response to World Hunger* (Minneapolis: Fortress Press, 2003).

Neufeld, Dietmar. "Jesus' Eating Transgressions and Social Impropriety in the Gospel of Mark: A Social Scientific Approach," *Biblical Theology Bulletin* 30:1 (Spring 2000): 15–26.

Portland's Bounty: A Guide to Eating Locally and Seasonally in the Greater Portland Area (Portland, Ore.: Interfaith Network for Earth Concerns/Ecumenical Ministries of Oregon, 1999).

Smith, Huston. "Reasons for Joy: The Soul of Christianity," *Christian Century* 122:30 (October 4, 2005): 10, 11.

Stull, Donald D., and Michael J. Broadway. *Slaughterhouse Blues: The Meat and Poultry Industry in North America* (Belmont, Calif.: Thomson/Wadsworth, 2004).

Stephen, Diana, ed. *We Are What We Eat* (Louisville, Ky: Presbyterian Church USA, 2002). Call 800-524-2612 and ask for # 68-600-02-003.

Worthington, Everett L., Suzanne E. Mazzeo, and Wendy L. Kliewer. "Addictive and Eating Disorders: Unforgiveness and Forgiveness," *Journal of Psychology and Christianity* 21:3 (Fall 2002): 257–61.

Zellner, Wendy. "The Wal-Mart of Meat," *Business Week* 3900 (September 20, 2004): 90–94.

Epilogue

Brown, Lester R. *Outgrowing the Earth: The Food Security Challenge in an Age of Falling Water Tables and Rising Temperatures* (New York: Norton, 2004).

Kristof, Nicholas D. "Waging a War We Can Be Proud Of," *New York Times*, January 10, 2006, A25.

Selected
Electronic Resources

Advocacy Organizations

Agricultural Missions, Inc.
www.agriculturalmissions.org
> Advocates for domestic and international groups, church-related and also
> educational; organizes tours by Third World peoples to witness to U.S. citizens

Community Food Security Coalition
www.foodsecurity.org
> Dedicated to building strong, sustainable, local and regional food systems that
> ensure access to affordable food in North America

Food First/Institute for Food and Development Policy
www.foodfirst.org
> Food and agriculture research organization founded by Frances Moore Lappe

Institute for Agriculture and Trade Policy
iatp@iatp.org
> Strong on both research and advocacy

National Campaign for Sustainable Agriculture
http://www.campaign@sustainableagriculture.net
> Advocacy and educational organization; supports policies that will promote
> healthy and equitable agriculture in the United States

Church-Related Organizations

Bread for the World

www.bread.org

> Advocacy organization that focuses on international development; historically a very strong advocate for attacking world hunger

Church of the Brethren:
General Board, Global Mission Partnerships

www.brethren.org/genbd/global_mission/index.htm

> Addresses world hunger concerns

Church World Service Disaster Response Program

www.cwserp.org

> Assists disaster survivors through interreligious organizations in the United States and worldwide

Ending Hunger Now

www.endinghungernow.org

> Set up by Fortress Press to extend the work of George McGovern, Bob Dole, and Donald E. Messer in *Ending Hunger Now* (2005)

Fair Food

www.pcusa.org/fairfood

> Run by the Presbyterian Church (USA), the United Church of Christ, and Pax Christi

Foods Resource Bank

www.foodsresourcebank.org

> Links rural and urban churches in growing food and then using the proceeds to fund global development organizations; contributes to congregational revitalization

Heifer International

www.heifer.org

> Development organization that uses animals to help people develop self-sustaining lifestyles internationally and domestically; excellent practice for children and youth to contribute toward the donation of animals

Lutheran World Federation

www.lutheranworld.org

Contributes theological study and action on hunger issues

National Catholic Rural Life Conference

www.ncrlc.com

Works closely with farmers, legislatures, and clergy; its Eating Is a Moral Act campaign is a good resource

National Council of Churches USA

www.ncccusa.org; search the word *hunger*.

Concerned with hunger, poverty, global issues, and protecting the earth

Practicing Our Faith, Valparaiso University

www.practicingourfaith.org

Focused on historic Christian practices; makes grants; special focus on youth practicing their faith

World Council of Churches

www.wcc-coe.org

International body comprised of Christian groups that focuses on hunger, disasters, theological interpretation, and justice issues

Educational Organizations

The Carsey Institute, University of New Hampshire

http://www.carseyinstitute.unh.edu

Research and educational organization that tracks food supply and rural issues

DayOne Publishing, CAMP System

http://www.mindfuleating.org/MindfulEating.html

Devoted to the benefits and process of mindful eating

Slow Food USA

http://www.slowfoodusa.org

U.S. branch of a global movement devoted to preparing and enjoying local foods and to relaxed and conscious eating

The True Cost Tour
http://www.truecosttour.org
   Walk people through a virtual grocery store

Fair Trade Organizations

For an introduction to fair trade products, visit **Global Exchange**,
   www.globalexchange.org, which includes a fair trade online store.

CASHEWS
Peacecraft, www.peacecraft.org
SERRV International, www.agreatergift.org

COFFEE
Bean North Coffee Roasting, www.beannorth.com
Café Campesino, www.cafecampesino.com
Earth Friendly Coffee, www.earthfriendlycoffee.com
Equal Exchange, Inc., www.equalexchange.com
Grounds for Change, www.groundsforchange.com
Higher Grounds Trading Company, www.javaforjustice.com
Just Coffee, www.justcoffee.net
Larry's Beans, www.larrysbeans.com
Mother Earth Coffee Company, www.motherearthcoffeeco.com
Peace Coffee, www.peacecoffee.com
Fair Trade Federation, www.fairtradefederation.org/memcof.html
TransFair USA, www.transfairusa.org

GOURMET GRAINS, HONEY, SALSA, CHOCOLATE BARS, SYRUP
SERRV International, www.agreatergift.org

HOT CHOCOLATE AND COCOA
Coco Camino, www.lasiembra.com
Equal Exchange, Inc., www.equalexchange.com
Global Exchange, www.globalexchange.org

TEA
Equal Exchange, Inc., www.equalexchange.com
SERRV International, www.agreatergift.org
TransFair USA, www.transfairusa.org

Governmental Organizations

Calorie Control Council
http://www.caloriecontrol.org
>Information on achieving and maintaining a healthy weight; consumer
>information on low-calorie, reduced-fat foods and beverages

Center for Food Safety and Applied Nutrition,
U.S. Food and Drug Administration
http://vm.cfsan.fda.gov/list.html
>Health and nutrition information related to food

The Food Timeline
http://www.foodtimeline.org/foodfaqa.html
>Helpful advice and tips about how to conduct research on particular foods

FoodFuture, Food and Drink Federation, United Kingdom
http://www.foodfuture.org.uk
>Seeks to provide a balanced account of the benefits and disadvantages of
>genetically modified foods

LocalHarvest
http://www.localharvest.org
>Provides a public directory of small farms nationwide aimed at helping
>consumers buy locally; helpful map zooms in to find specific locations

National Agriculture Library, U.S. Department of Agriculture
http://www.nutrition.gov
>Information about nutrition and healthy eating; links to government programs
>such as Food Stamps, WIC (Women, Infants, and Children), and School Lunch
>and Breakfast

Nutrient Database for Standard Reference,
U.S. Department of Agriculture
http://www.nal.usda.gov/fnic/foodcomp/search/
>Find out the makeup and nutritional content of your favorite foods in detail

Local Food Organizations

CONNECTICUT
Hartford Food System, www.hartfordfood.org

ILLINOIS
Growing Power, www.growingpower.org

MINNESOTA
Minnesota Grown, www.mda.state.mn.us/mngrown

MISSOURI
Food Circles Networking Project, www.foodcircles.missouri.edu/vision.htm

NEW YORK CITY
Council on the Environment of New York City, www.cenyc.org

SAN FRANCISCO, CA
Center for Urban Eduction about Sustainable Agriculture,
www.ferryplazafarmersmarket.com

UNITED STATES
The Food Trust, www.thefoodtrust.org
FoodRoutes Network, www.foodroutes.org
LocalHarvest, www.localharvest.org

VANCOUVER, CANADA
FarmFolk/CityFolk Society, www.ffcf.bc.ca

VERMONT
The Vermont Fresh Network, www.vermontfresh.net

WISCONSIN
Growing Power, www.growingpower.org

Name and Subject Index

Printed in the United States
132739LV00006B/20/P